How to
INTERPRET
DREAMS
and
VISIONS

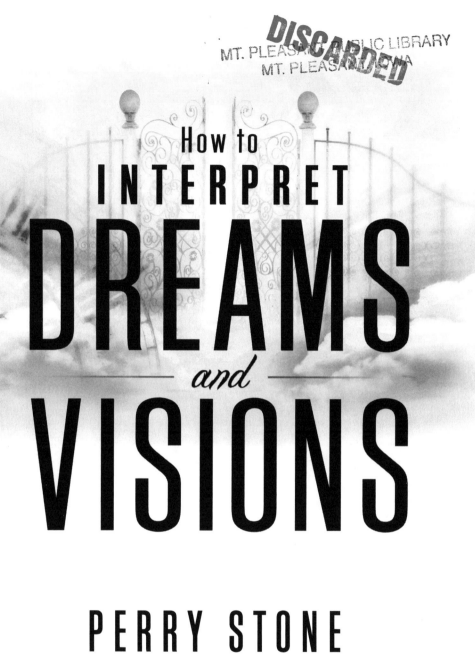

How to
INTERPRET
DREAMS
and
VISIONS

PERRY STONE

CHARISMA
HOUSE

Most Charisma House Book Group products are available at special quantity discounts for bulk purchase for sales promotions, premiums, fund-raising, and educational needs. For details, write Charisma House Book Group, 600 Rinehart Road, Lake Mary, Florida 32746, or telephone (407) 333-0600.

How to Interpret Dreams and Visions by Perry Stone
Published by Charisma House
Charisma Media/Charisma House Book Group
600 Rinehart Road
Lake Mary, Florida 32746
www.charismahouse.com

Unless otherwise noted, all Scripture quotations are from the New King James Version of the Bible. Copyright © 1979, 1980, 1982 by Thomas Nelson, Inc., publishers. Used by permission.

Scripture quotations marked AMP are from the Amplified Bible. Old Testament copyright © 1965, 1987 by the Zondervan Corporation. The Amplified New Testament copyright © 1954, 1958, 1987 by the Lockman Foundation. Used by permission.

Scripture quotations marked KJV are from the King James Version of the Bible.

Scripture quotations marked NIV are from the Holy Bible, New International Version. Copyright © 1973, 1978, 1984, International Bible Society. Used by permission.

Cover design by Justin Evans
Design Director: Bill Johnson

Visit the author's website at www.voe.org.

Library of Congress Cataloging-in-Publication Data:
Stone, Perry F.
  How to interpret dreams and visions / Perry Stone.
      p. cm.
  Includes bibliographical references (p.   ).
  ISBN 978-1-61638-350-3
1. Dreams--Religious aspects--Christianity. 2. Dream interpretation. 3.
Visions. I. Title.
  BR115.D74S76 2011
  248.2'9--dc22
                                          2010053909

E-book ISBN: 978-1-61638-426-5

14 15 16 17 18 — 9 8 7 6 5 4
Printed in the United States of America

DEDICATION

It is only fitting that I dedicate this book to the man who has had the greatest influence upon my life and ministry, my father, Fred Stone. Dad's life and ministry have been of impeccable integrity. He was recognized among his peers as a spiritual, praying man who believed that the Lord still spoke to His children—through the Word of God and through the manifestations of the Holy Spirit. From the time he was a teenager, God visited him in both visions and dreams, many times to warn individuals of coming danger and at other times to bring a word of wisdom in assisting a believer through a time of crisis. Throughout this book I will share some of the remarkable visitations he received to illustrate key points as revealed in Scripture.

On several occasions Dad's dreams have saved the lives of family members as they heeded each warning he gave and were guided by what he said. The same anointing for seeing spiritual warnings in dreams and visions began marking my own life as a young minister. Since the Bible indicates that in the last days God will visit us through dreams and visions, we need a full understanding of this method of receiving revelation from heaven and how to understand the messages from our heavenly Father. May the insight from these pages open a new avenue of knowledge and understanding of how God warns, leads, and guides our steps, and how He reveals His concern about our protection, direction, and spiritual wisdom for daily living.

CONTENTS

Introduction 1

1 The Last Days—Time to Pierce the Veil 9

2 The Dream Factor 23

3 Why Are Some Dreams Delayed in Coming to Pass? 35

4 Nightmares and Dirty Dreaming 53

5 False Prophets and False Dreams 69

6 The Psychic Voices Versus the Prophetic Visions 83

7 Can a Warning Dream Be Altered Through Prayer? 99

8 Learning to Listen to Your Wife's Warning Dreams 105

9 What It Means When Dreaming of
a Departed Loved One 119

10 The Law of the Double Dream 137

11 Angel Appearances in Dreams 145

12 Why the Symbolism—Can't God Make It Plain? 159

13 Four Types of Spiritual Visions 179

14 Dreams—Amazing Purpose for These Revelations 189

Conclusion: Dreams and Visions—
God's Voice of Intimacy 207

Appendix: Detailed Biblical Symbolism in Dreams 213

Notes 237

INTRODUCTION

In June of 1996 I had a spiritual experience that later proved to be a warning of a future terrorist attack upon America. I was ministering at the Assembly of God in Brooksville, Florida, and was eating dinner at a local member's home on a beautiful Sunday afternoon. After eating, I was suddenly overwhelmed with a feeling of extreme tiredness, so I excused myself from the table to lie down and rest. It was about three o'clock when I lay across the bed, attempting to read my Bible. Within minutes I laid my head on the Bible and immediately went into a very deep sleep.

My very brief sleep was abruptly interrupted by a full-color vision! I was standing at the bottom of a paved road, looking up toward the top of a hill where the road ended at a large concrete wall. There were red-brick, one-story homes on the left and right sides of the road, with sidewalks climbing the hill on either side. Just above the wall in a clear blue sky I saw a black cloud that was a perfect square. I was curious as to what this was, so I began walking up the left sidewalk toward the top of the hill. I noticed I was barefoot, which I later learned was an indication in a dream of not being prepared for what was coming.

I climbed on top of the wall and saw a strange sight. It was a large cornfield with rows of full-grown corn. As I looked from left to right, it appeared endless. However, it was several hundreds yards across in front of me. Directly in the center at the end of the field was a large tower-looking building, the exact form of the World Trade Center in New York. It was shrouded in a solid black cloud from the top to the bottom. The more frightening part was the five grayish, spinning tornadoes that were appearing to form in front of this large tower. The tornadoes were motionless, but suddenly the left one began spinning violently, throwing sparks and other objects out from it. It was as though the second one received its strength from the first one, and soon all five were emitting sparks, spinning with great grayish smoke. I distinctly remember they were not black as normal tornadoes are.

As the left one began spinning, it moved from in front of the tower into the cornfield and began ripping corn out by the roots, leaving an empty straight path. The other four were preparing to move in the same manner—each destroying a line of corn from the back to the front of the corn in the field. That is when I turned, running down the hill yelling, "We must get into the cleft of the rock..." I repeated the same phrase twice.

I suddenly realized I was lying on the bed and my eyes were open. I was so overwhelmed, not knowing what I had witnessed, that I left the room to speak with a fellow minister, Don Channel, who was traveling with me. I told him the vision and said the tower looked like the World Trade Center shrouded in black, but I was uncertain as to what it meant. That night I informed the church what I saw and immediately began sharing the vision with others. The interpretation was unclear—as often happens in a spiritual warning. The understanding either must be prayed about or will be understood as the vision begins to unfold. For several years I told the vision, and in 1999 an artist, J. Michael Leonard, drew a sketch of what I described to him in the vision. He also drew a picture of a second vision I experienced months later, which I felt tied into this one.

THE SECOND VISITATION

Months later I experienced a second vision that involved five gray tornadoes. This time I was in a large city and began to hear people screaming, "The storm is coming; what should we do?" I led them into a downtown church constructed from large grayish stones. I saw three ethnic groups: African American, Hispanic, and Asian men and women all huddled together with their ethnic groups. Some were in shock, and others were in prayer.

Looking through an opening of the church door, I saw five grayish tornadoes, one following another, spinning wildly. This time there were soda cans, computer paper, and all sorts of debris being thrown from the rolling and spinning gray clouds. A total of five tornadoes passed by. When we went outside, there were intact downtown office buildings that were sitting empty, the offices ruined and incapable of conducting business. The entire city was stunned, and outsiders were setting up areas on the streets with food, water, clothes, and even children's toys for those within the city who had experienced some form of destruction from these storms.

I knew these two visions were linked; however, the understanding was uncertain. When I shared these two visions with partners at our main meeting in Pigeon Forge, Tennessee, later that year, I told them I believed there would be a major terrorist attack on the World Trade Center at some point in the future. After showing the drawings in 1999 during a national prophetic television special and still nothing had happened, I put the sketches in my office closet at work and said nothing further about them—until the morning of September 4, 2001. While cleaning the closet, I pulled the drawings out and told a coworker in our office, Mel Colbeck, "Mel, this is a terror attack coming against the World Trade Center in the future. I don't know when, but it will happen!"

THEN CAME 9/11

On the morning of September 11, 2001, I was working at our ministry center in the *Manna-Fest* order fulfillment room when my secretary ran in and announced, "Someone has flown a plane into the World Trade Center." I was thinking that a small plane had struck the tower when a pilot died in flight. Within a few moments she said, "A second plane was flown into the second tower, and it is believed to be a terrorist attack." That is when the reality of the five-year-old vision hit me! I went home, and on the television screen I saw the black smoke from the first plane pouring upward, forming that black square I saw in the vision. Later, when both towers collapsed, I witnessed the fulfillment of the vision with the *gray smoke* rolling down the street, being described by news commentators as a "tornado," sending multitudes running into buildings for safety. I would later learn from ground zero workers that many people also found refuge in a large church called Trinity Church, seeking safety and praying. It was the exact description of the building and activity occurring within the church I had seen in the second vision.

At that moment, the meaning of five tornadoes was not making sense. I thought there would be five attacks (the Pentagon, the plane crash in Pennsylvania, and perhaps one more making five). However, within forty-eight hours it was clear. Trade centers one and two, the twin towers, were attacked, resulting in the eventual destruction of trade center buildings three, four, five, six, and seven—five other buildings housing thousands of businesses. Other office complexes were ruined by the dust and were closed. Of course there were many relief organizations bringing food, water, and needed resources to both the people in need and the workers at ground zero. What about the cornfield?

In the story of Joseph, the cornfield represented a famine coming to Egypt. The 9/11 attacks did not disrupt food. However, corn in the Old Testament was a staple that was also sold and was a vital part of the economy of the ancient world. In the New Testament parables, the field represents the world, and the corn (wheat) the harvest. Looking back in retrospect, the trade center was the *World* Trade Center with offices representing numerous nations housed within the towers (thus the field—the *world*). Also, corn can represent the economy, and the 9/11 attacks had a devastating impact not only on New York City but also upon the travel industry in general. Thus the corn was *rooted up*, indicating that those in these five buildings would no longer have jobs in those buildings! I later realized that the concrete wall from which I viewed the storms may have been an allusion to *Wall Street*, which was not impacted by the storms in the manner that the other buildings were. Getting in the *cleft of the rock* was a direct reference to Christ, who is the rock of our salvation and a shelter in the time of storm.

WHAT ABOUT YOUR DREAMS OR VISIONS?

Have you ever dreamed a dream that was quite troubling and it remained with you for many days? Have you ever experienced a full-color vision while sleeping—one that is so vivid that you can smell fragrances and feel the cool wind brushing your face? It is possible that your dream has a spiritual connotation and that your vision is definitely some form of a message from the presence of the Almighty.

We humans have difficulty interpreting the meanings of a spiritual dream or vision, as they often contain unique or unusual symbolism. Why does God often use symbolism and not allow us to comprehend a simple, plain meaning for the interpretation? What does the symbolism mean? How can you know if a night encounter seen during your sleep is from the Lord and not just the apparition of a wild imagination? In this book I have detailed biblical insight to assist the reader in understanding the answers to these and many more questions.

It was the Lord Himself who proclaimed in a biblical prophecy that in the last days He would pour out His Spirit upon all flesh, with one major result being that "young men shall see visions...old men shall dream dreams" (Acts 2:17). If the Holy Spirit is going to give to the body of Christ heavenly warnings, divine revelations, and practical instructions through visions or dreams, then believers must be well informed about the methods and meanings of these special and unique manifestations. This is what this book is all about.

All of the best for you and your family,

—PERRY STONE
Founder of Voice of Evangelism and Host of *Manna-Fest*

THE LAST DAYS—
TIME TO PIERCE THE VEIL

But their minds were blinded. For until this day the same veil remains unlifted in the reading of the Old Testament, because the veil is taken away in Christ. But even to this day, when Moses is read, a veil lies on their heart. Nevertheless when one turns to the Lord, the veil is taken away. Now the Lord is the Spirit; and where the Spirit of the Lord is, there is liberty.

« 2 Corinthians 3:14–17 »

The spirit world is as real as the air we breathe and the water we drink. The natural realm is a reflection of the spirit world. Earthly things are patterned after heavenly things. (See Hebrews 8:1–5.) Our world consists of trees, rivers, mountains, and cities. The heavenly city, New Jerusalem, has the tree of life, the crystal river of life, and a mountain where God is worshiped called *Mount Zion* (Rev. 22:1–5). These heavenly realities were the original Creation that was reflected on Earth when God created man.

Humanity has struggled to believe in a world that cannot be seen with the eyes, touched with the hands, or smelled when we breathe. To the skeptic, angels are myths, and demonic spirits are the dark imagination of Hollywood scripts. The prevailing attitude is the *Thomas syndrome,* which says, "Unless I can see it and touch it, I will never believe it" (John 20:25, author's paraphrase). The fact is that there is an invisible veil covering both the natural eyes and the spiritual understanding of men and women, and only when the veil is lifted or *pierced* can the realities of the invisible realm become visible. The Bible is a book written by forty different authors over a period of about fifteen hundred years of time that tells the story of men called *prophets* who were inspired of the Lord and who pierced this veil and saw marvelous eternal and heavenly images that brought to mankind the revelation of God.

Paul wrote that there is a veil, similar to scales, over the eyes of our understanding that clouds the light of God's revelation from entering into our minds and enlightening us with life-changing insight. If we live behind this veil, then we will never know or experience God's best for us. This veil, which at times manifests as a lack of interest in spiritual matters, a dullness in our understanding, or a spirit of unbelief toward the idea of Bible-based spiritual manifestations, *must be lifted* to experience the unseen. This ability to see the future was the gift that set apart the biblical prophets from their false counterparts in surrounding idolatrous nations. These Hebrew visionaries had a reputation for knowing the unknown behind closed doors.

One such example can be seen when a Syrian general sent his army to capture one of God's prophets, Elisha. When Elisha's servant saw the army, fear gripped him. However, after Elisha prayed for the eyes of his servant to be opened, the fear turned to faith as the servant saw horses and chariots of fire encamped round about them both, forming a protective hedge. (See 2 Kings 6:8–17.) There is a covering of some sort on our physical eyes, which prevents us from seeing the activity of the spirit world. However, when we sleep, we are still able to *see* images through dreams or visions. In Scripture, men like the apostle John recorded these dreams and visions. John was on an island when he suddenly saw a "door in heaven open," or as we would say, "heaven open," and this opening projected his mind and spirit into another world, a world just as real as the world we live in. (See Revelation 4:1; 19:11.) These two biblical incidents from Revelation indicate two important facts: something occurs on Earth and something occurs in heaven to cause information to be released and the veil removed. On Earth our eyes must be "opened." This happens when our inner vision, which creates the images in our brain at night, receives information from the heavenly realm, which "opens," allowing eternal information to pass from the heavenly realm to the earthly realm.

One question posed by sincere seekers is: "Why would God be concerned about revealing events to us that have not yet occurred?" A simple answer is that He does so to prepare us for something or to cause us to intercede in prayer to prevent or to change a situation. For example, when King Hezekiah was informed by Isaiah to set his house in order because he would soon die, the king began to earnestly pray, and his death was delayed for fifteen years (Isa. 38:1–5).

Another reason God is concerned is because He knows we need to understand certain events in the future.

WHY IS THE SPIRIT WORLD VEILED?

Human eyes cannot see into the spirit world. God is a Spirit (John 4:24). Angels are spirits (Heb. 1:13–14). Satan's kingdom is organized into four levels of spirit rebels (Eph. 6:12), and every man is a tripartite creation of a body, a soul, and a spirit, or, as some teach, a spirit with a soul living in a body (1 Thess. 5:23).

In the time of Adam and Eve, God entered the Garden of Eden and communicated directly with man by walking through the garden in the cool of the day (Gen. 3:8). Adam and Eve could see and hear God clearly. After they fell into sin, "the eyes of both of them were opened," and they saw they were naked and felt shame (Gen. 3:7). Although their eyes were opened, at the same time their eyes were veiled. From that moment forward, angelic visitors appeared in the form of a vision, a dream, or would take upon themselves human form, just as the two angelic messengers did when instructed by the Almighty to investigate the sins of Sodom. (See Genesis 19.) Even the writer of Hebrews wrote to be careful when entertaining a stranger because you might not be aware that it is an angel (Heb. 13:2).

If our eyes could be opened and the veil lifted, we would continually see angels, demonic entities, and other forms of spirit beings. While some may wish to see into the invisible realm, the fact is that when great men of God and Hebrew prophets have pierced this veil and seen, for example, angels in their full glory, the reactions have normally been to fall down and be gripped with an overwhelming feeling of fear. Abraham fell into a deep trance (Gen. 15:12) and fell on his face when God talked to him (Gen. 17:3, 17). Ezekiel describes seeing the Almighty upon His throne, with cherubim and amazing heavenly beings appearing like wheels spinning within wheels

(Ezek. 1), and he too fell upon his face (v. 28). In several instances when a vision of God or the angelic realm manifested, the prophet fell down upon his face (Ezek. 9:8; 43:3; 44:4). Daniel described an angelic visitor with brass-colored arms and feet, white hair, a gold belt, and eyes like fire. His reaction was so visibly powerful that even the men with him who did not see the vision became overwhelmed and began "quaking" and fled, hiding themselves (Dan. 10:5–7, kjv). Daniel found himself on his face with no strength remaining in his body (vv. 8–9). When John saw the resurrected Christ in heaven, he "fell at His feet as dead" (Rev. 1:17). Even Balaam's donkey fell down when it saw an angel of the Lord (Num. 22:27)!

When the veil is lifted and a mere mortal taps into not just a vision or dream, but into the actual unseen world of angels, demons, heaven, or hell, the human body is unable to sustain the glory of the heavenly realm without responding in some manner. If we could live with our spiritual eyes continually opened, I suggest we would never get any work done and would be continually disrupted in our sleep.

Scripture instructs believers to "walk by faith, not by sight" (2 Cor. 5:7). I cannot physically see God, but I believe in God because of the Bible's evidence and because I have faith that undergirds my confidence in the Word. With my human eyes I am unable to spot an angel flying through the heavens or a cosmic conflict between warring angels and prince spirits called the "spiritual hosts of wickedness in the heavenly places" (Eph. 6:12). However, because my inner being is also a "spirit," I can at times sense or *feel* the presence of the Lord, the warmth and peace of an angel, or the dark oppressive wicked spirits that are in my earth zone. To pierce the curtain of the unseen, a believer must be *in tune* to that particular realm of spiritual activity.

THERE IS A FUTURE

When my seventy-seven-year-old father was praying for my twenty-year-old son, who was kneeling before him at Dad's small home in Tennessee, with tears in his eyes my father said to Jonathan, "There is a future." He was encouraging his grandson not to just live for the *moment* but to discover, plan, and prevail for his future, which the Lord has already laid out for him and his little sister. At that moment I realized that this is what life is really all about—the future. When God laid out a detailed plan for man's redemption from sin, He prepared the details long before Adam fell. Jesus is called "the Lamb slain from the foundation of the world" (Rev. 13:8). When Christ was praying before His death, He said that God had loved Him from "before the foundation of the world" (John 17:24). *God planned a future for all of mankind before Adam and Eve were created and fell into sin!*

Once man sinned, God Himself released the first prophecy by predicting that the seed of the woman would bruise the head of the serpent (Gen. 3:15). God spoke this about four thousand years before Mary gave birth to the Messiah (Luke 2). After Cain slew his brother, Abel, God wasted no time in replacing Abel with Adam and Eve's new addition to the family, a son named Seth who would initiate a nine-generation lineage of righteous men, leading up to tenth man from Adam, Noah. (See Genesis 5.) *God continually has your future on His mind and in His purpose.*

The Almighty's passion for the future is also witnessed in the fact that God thinks generationally. When God established His covenant through Abraham, He was planning that Abraham's descendants would become a nation. First God promised Abraham a son and to make a "great nation" from Abraham's children (Gen. 12:2). Years later God predicted that Abraham would be "a great and mighty nation" (Gen. 18:18). Years passed, and then God visited Abraham's grandson Jacob, changing his name from *Jacob* to *Israel*. God enlarged His promise by saying to Jacob, "A nation and a company of nations shall proceed from you" (Gen. 35:11). After the nation of Israel expanded from seventy souls to more than six hundred thousand men of war (Exod. 1:5; 12:37), the Lord announced that the nation would be "blessed above all peoples" (Deut. 7:14). From one simple individual, Abraham, to seventy souls who went into Egypt under Joseph, in four hundred years the nation grew to six hundred thousand men marching through the Red Sea and on to the millions of Jewish people now in the world. God was beginning the preparations for one large family called the *children of Israel* when He was making covenant with one man—Abraham! This is why God changed Abram's name (meaning "father") to Abraham, meaning "father of many" (Gen. 17:5). Israel began with a dream and a vision!

PIERCING THE VEIL

Securing confidence and boldness for the future is so significant to the Almighty that He allowed men to enter into the dream dimension and receive vital knowledge for themselves, for their leaders, or for the nations in which they were given authority. A few examples of significant dreams that altered situations, set destinies, or brought prophetic knowledge are:

- ► God warned King Abimelech with the threat of death if he didn't return Sarah to Abraham (Gen. 20:6–7).

- ► God confirmed in a dream for Jacob to leave Laban, taking his wives and sons to Canaan (Gen. 31).

- ► God prepared Joseph's future by giving him two prophetic dreams when he was a teenager (Gen. 37).

- ▶ God allowed Joseph to interpret the dreams of the butler and the baker while in prison (Gen. 40).

- ▶ Joseph interpreted both dreams of Pharaoh and prepared for a seven-year famine (Gen. 41).

- ▶ It was the "barley cake dream" that gave Gideon confidence to fight the Midianites (Judg. 7).

- ▶ God appeared to Solomon in a dream, granting his request for the gift of wisdom (1 Kings 3).

- ▶ Daniel was the only man in Babylon capable of interpreting the dream of the metallic image (Dan. 2).

- ▶ Daniel later interpreted Nebuchadnezzar's "tree dream," predicting the downfall of the king (Dan. 4).

- ▶ Daniel experienced a major prophetic dream of world empires symbolized by wild beasts (Dan. 7).

Nearly six thousand years of human history have demonstrated that just because God plans a person's future, it is no guarantee that opposition will not eclipse the light of the revelation. There is a plan by the kingdom of darkness to distract, disrupt, and destroy the future, both God's prophetic plan and your personal destiny. Each person is said to have a "destiny," which is simply *your future according to God.* Just as God revealed to Jeremiah that He foreknew him when he was still in his mother's womb and that He preordained him to be a prophet (Jer. 1:5), God has a predetermined plan for each person. With all of the clutter and clamor and mixed voices speaking into our lives, our minds can become cloudy and our understanding fogged with numerous possibilities from which we must choose. This is why at times God will permit a believer to pierce the world of the natural and enter the realm of a dream or a vision so that secret strategies of the enemy can be exposed and the hidden plans of God can be revealed. Warnings that are perceived and received can help you avoid potholes and pits in your path to destiny, and understanding God's plan will empower you to pursue that purpose.

The disrupting of God's will in our lives can begin at a very early age. During major prophetic cycles and seasons of prophetic fulfillment, children come under severe attack from the adversary. This was seen when Pharaoh ordered the male infants born to the Hebrews to be cast into the Nile River (Exod. 1:22). The time was coming when a deliverer would bring the Hebrews out of Egypt, and the adversary was no doubt attempting to preempt the prophecy by killing the possible male child deliverer before he could become a man! The second assignment of an evil ruler was when Herod commissioned Roman soldiers to encircle the area of Ramah and kill all male children who were under two years of age, attempting to slay the future king of the Jews that the wise men came to worship (Matt. 2).

From a personal perspective, if we survive our birth and live to be teenagers, other battles begin. When he was a teenager (age seventeen), a plot was organized against Joseph by his own brothers (Gen. 37). They were sick of this dreamer, Daddy's favorite little spoiled boy, running around with an expensive coat! Joseph was doing well until he began to confess his dreams of success that would come to him. At that point his brothers conspired against him, and Joseph ended up in a pit, then in a prison, and spent thirteen years in what seemed negative, *dream-killing* circumstances.

I was a young teenager when the Lord began to reveal to me His will and I began planning for it. I encountered various types of verbal persecution from my own spiritual brothers in the same denomination of which I was a member. When David—just a teen—was anointed by Samuel as the next king "in the midst of his brothers," jealousy arose among certain brothers much older who may have felt they deserved the position more than their kid brother (1 Sam. 16:13; 17:28).

When I was a teenager, the Holy Spirit inspired me to organize a ministry called Voice of Evangelism when I had only preached in three states. Ministers said, "Perry isn't the voice of anything, much less of evangelism." They were correct from the natural perspective but wrong in the Spirit. The Lord had a future for me! At age eighteen I formed a "7-Point Outreach Plan" that included a ministry outreach through books, revival meetings, magazines, and other forms of branching out. Then I began overhearing statements like: "Who does he think he is, Billy Graham or Oral Roberts?" Without sounding arrogant, I knew something these other men did not know. I had a small glimpse into the future. I had both heard and seen in my spirit and through dreams and prayer that I would be used of the Lord to one day have a worldwide ministry. *Thus, once you see your future, you can learn how to hold off the adversity and know why there is opposition against your destiny!*

WATCH OUT FOR THAT GIRL

When my father, Fred Stone, was a young, black-haired teenage minister, he met a very attractive girl about his age who was gifted in playing the piano and singing. Of course, the common belief was that if you were a minister, your wife needed to be a singer or musician. The girl took a liking to him. However, Dad had a dream in which he saw this girl coming out of a barn embracing a young man. He realized the girl was having relations with this boy. He heard a voice say, "I have warned you; have nothing to do with that girl." Dad said that after this dream, the girl tried to get close to him in friendship; he would say hello but go no further. Even Dad's uncle, a noted minister, rebuked Dad for not expressing more interest in such a talented young girl. But three months later the girl's father told Dad's uncle he was glad Dad had not formed a relationship with his daughter, because she was pregnant out of wedlock by a fellow she knew.

When I was the same age as my father, a similar situation was repeated in my life. I was eighteen years of age, traveling from church to church conducting weekly revivals. At one location, a family I knew with a daughter about my age wanted me to go out with her to eat. My policy was to only go out with a group of young people and avoid going out alone with the opposite sex. Soon she began to speak to friends that she was serious about me and thought our friendship could lead to eventual marriage. At the same time I dreamed that she was pregnant. In the dream the Lord told me to avoid her. The same week, three noted ministers spoke to me in confidence and said, "You must be careful around this girl. There is something not right about her." I sent word to her through a friend not to have any contact with me again. One month later it was confirmed that she was pregnant, and she married the father of the child shortly thereafter. Years later she and her mother came to hear me minister in a church and asked to speak with me. Her mother, a very godly woman, required her to apologize to me for plotting to pull me into her situation without my knowledge. The girl said, "I was hoping you would suddenly fall in love with me and marry me before anyone knew I was pregnant with this man's baby."

In both cases, more than twenty-six years apart, the same type of snare was laid for Dad and me. By following the same type of dreams and inward warnings, we both avoided missing the will of God and entering into a situation that would have been not only questionable but also embarrassing and detrimental to our early ministries. These illustrations reveal how strategies are set to disrupt God's purposes, but God is concerned about the details of our personal lives because *circumstances* affect our destiny!

Often when we think of a spiritual dream we envision a visitation that warns us of national calamity or an international warning on the same level as what the Old Testament prophets received when warning the priests and the kings of coming calamity. However, God has indicated in Scripture that He is concerned for each individual and not just for the collective population of a nation. Christ revealed that the Father watched a sparrow fall to the ground and saw the lilies in the field grow (Matt. 10:29; Luke 12:28), and if the Almighty is concerned for the smallest in His creation, how much more is His concern manifested toward man, who is made in His image (Gen. 1:26).

THE NEED TO KNOW

The understanding of the Book of Daniel was sealed "until the time of the end," when "knowledge shall increase" (Dan. 12:4). Numerous prophecies are assigned to occur in the "time of the end," a term used in the Book of Daniel five times (Dan. 8:17; 11:35, 40; 12:4, 9). Other predictions will unfold in the "last days," a phrase coined to identify the time frame prior to the return of the Messiah, listed five times in the New Testament (Acts 2:17; 2 Tim. 3:1; Heb. 1:2; James 5:3; 2 Pet. 3:3). The final outpouring of the Holy Spirit will occur in the "last days" (Acts 2:17) and includes sons and daughters prophesying and experiencing visions and dreams. Among this final generation there is a *need-to-know* attitude about their future and destiny.

This *need to know* is obvious when one considers the millions of dollars spent by sincere yet uninformed individuals on fortune-tellers, astrologers, séances, and psychics. According to the Pew Forum for Religion and Public Life, "about 1 in 7 Americans consulted a psychic or fortune teller in 2009."[1] The only reason these false prophets of greed are consulted is to determine the hidden and the unseen and to know in advance the person's future. Why should the body of Christ sit back and refuse to tell this generation to seek God for His direction, when the adversary will provide a horoscope for that purpose? There is a human need to know, and our knowledge for redemption can be found in the Bible—as well as the guide for practical living found in those inspired Scriptures. However, there are times we are uncertain concerning personal and national decisions that can be seen and understood through visions and dreams. However, the invisible veil must be pierced in the mind and in the understanding. This begins with the "dream factor."

two

THE DREAM FACTOR

Then He said, "Hear now My words: If there is a prophet among you, I, the LORD, make Myself known unto him in a vision; I speak to him in a dream."

« Numbers 12:6 »

It was approximately 2,500 years after the creation of Adam that God came to Moses in the wilderness and revealed the first written record of God's Word to mankind. From Adam to Noah's flood is about ten generations, stretching for 1,658 years. From Noah's son Shem to the arrival of Abraham is another ten generations and a span of several hundred years (Gen. 11:10–26). These years are called by theologians the *dispensation of human government*, as mankind had no written law to turn to and follow. God, however, did not remain silent for 2,500 years. He began revealing His will through dreams, visions, angelic encounters, and even personal visitations from Himself. When a righteous man or a patriarch such as Abraham, Isaac, Jacob, or Joseph dreamed a spiritual dream, there was always a cryptic message encoded in the dream or the symbolism thereof.

In the Bible, dreaming dreams is referred to 115 times, and the word *vision* is used 79 times in the English translation of the Bible. Some suggest that since we have the Bible, there is no longer any need for God to speak through a dream or a vision. However, the Bible itself is clear that as God pours out His Spirit in the last days, the visitations from heaven will be accompanied by both visions and dreams:

> And it shall come to pass in the last days, says God,
> That I will pour out of My Spirit on all flesh;
> Your sons and your daughters shall prophesy,
> Your young men shall see visions,
> Your old men shall dream dreams.
> And on My menservants and on My maidservants
> I will pour out My Spirit in those days;
> And they shall prophesy.
>
> —ACTS 2:17–18

Since dreams and visions are going to be manifested through believers as the Holy Spirit begins flowing throughout the earth in the last days, then we need to be made aware of these two methods of delivering messages, warnings, and instructions and know how to correctly read or interpret the meanings of the dreams and visions.

THE ACT OF DREAMING

There are two types of people: those who dream often and those who seldom dream. I am definitely a nightly dreamer, and my wife seldom, if ever, dreams—or if she does, she doesn't remember the content. At some point all people will experience a dream. Most dreams are a visual mental screen that moves from scene to scene while we sleep. Very few dreams can actually be classified as a spiritual dream, although there have been noted psychologists and researchers who believe every dream may have some type of a hidden meaning through the symbolism.

When believers begin experiencing dreams that hold a cryptic or hidden warning and message, the act of dreaming can be applied to three different categories.

First is the occasional dream that has an important message. As stated, I dream continually throughout the night, but my lovely wife, Pam, seldom dreams. However, if she tells you she had a strange dream, the probability is about nine out of ten that her dream is a message or a particular warning.

The second category relates to dreamers who have a natural gift for seeing future events, which is quite unexplainable. Among the ancient prophetic empires—Egypt, Babylon, Persia, and Greece— when the ruling kings had a troubling dream, they assembled the "wise men" or "seers" from their kingdom to interpret the meaning or give instructions (Gen. 41:8; Dan. 2:2). In most instances these men had a particular gift of wisdom and understanding, even though many if not all were worshipers of strange gods (such as with the case with the magicians of Pharaoh, in Exodus 7:11, and the wise men of Babylon). It is interesting to note that when God gave Pharaoh and Nebuchadnezzar prophetic dreams, not one of the seers, dream interpreters, or wise men in their kingdoms could receive the understanding of the symbolism in the prophetic dream. Only two men filled with the Spirit of the Lord, Joseph and Daniel, could understand the meanings! This fact reveals that God never intends for the so-called "sons of this world" (Luke 16:8) to understand spiritual mysteries. He gives revelation about spiritual mysteries only to men (or women) who have the spirit of wisdom and understanding through the Holy Spirit (Eph. 1:17–18).

The third category of dreamers are those who have received a special gift of revelation and illumination. In Scripture, Jacob, the son of Isaac, was a dreamer of dreams and experienced a dramatic dream of angels ascending and descending from a ladder whose base was upon the earth and whose top was positioned at the gate of heaven (Gen. 28:12–19). Apparently this "dreaming gift" was transferred to Jacob's favorite son, Joseph, who at age seventeen dreamed two distinct dreams indicating that all of his brothers would one day bow before him (Gen. 37:5–10). Joseph irritated his jealous brothers with his exciting revelation, bringing him mockery and eventually landing him in a pit and then leading to his being sold to a group of slave-purchasing nomads! Notice the reaction of his brothers and his father when Joseph shared his dream: "His brothers envied him, but his father kept the matter in mind" (v. 11).

This is the difference between someone who is *carnally* minded and someone who is *spiritually* minded. The brothers had never experienced a dream of their own with any meaning, but their father, Jacob, had on several occasions. No doubt Jacob saw the same type of *anointing* upon his son Joseph, even though one part of Joseph's dream made little sense. Joseph saw the eleven stars, sun, and moon bowing before him. We know there were twelve sons of Jacob if we include Joseph, and there are twelve major constellations in the main circuit that the sun moves through during a solar year. The eleven stars were not eleven single stars somewhere in the heaven, but these eleven stars alluded to the eleven different major star constellations in the heavens. Joseph's father, Jacob, interpreted the dream to mean that the stars were Joseph's brothers, the sun was Jacob, and the moon was Joseph's mother (Gen. 37:10). All eleven brothers and the father were living, but Joseph's mother, Rachel, had died giving birth to Benjamin some years prior (Gen. 35:18–19). Rachel gave birth to only two sons—Joseph and Benjamin. Rachel was Jacob's favorite wife, and these two boys were very special to him. However, Momma was now dead. It would be literally impossible for her to be the symbol of the moon and to bow down to Joseph, and I am certain this is why Jacob did not search out the full interpretation of Joseph's double dream but instead pondered it. Some of the dream—at the time— didn't make sense.

One thing I have learned over many years of ministry as it deals with God sending you an instruction using a dream or vision is that there are times when certain parts of what you see are not completely understood at that moment. What you see in the dream can be explained and is clear and certain, but your *understanding* of the events or what they mean can be fallible within your own interpretation. I almost made this mistake years after seeing the vision of the World Trade Center shrouded in the black cloud. The vision took place in 1996. In 1999, however, when I was showing the drawings of the vision that had been done by an artist who illustrated what appeared to be the World Trade Center shrouded in black (see drawings earlier in this book), a computer mainframe expert said, "Perry, that tall object may be a tall computer mainframe that could be impacted by the Y2K computer glitch that some are saying may occur at midnight of the first day of 2000." I looked at the picture and said, "I always thought it looked like the World Trade Center, but maybe you're right!" In 1999 I hosted a major prophetic special program that was aired on national television, showing the various drawings of the warning vision from 1996. I mentioned it could be a terrorist attack but *added*, "Perhaps it is a computer mainframe." From 1996 to 2001, every day at some time I thought about what I saw but could not put it all together—until the day of September 11, 2001, when it was made clear.

In a strong spiritual visitation in which you see something that is a warning, do not be discouraged or frustrated if you do not always comprehend or understand the events 100 percent. It is written, "It is the glory of God to conceal a matter, but the glory of kings is to search out a matter" (Prov. 25:2). The searching out of something hidden was the process Daniel used when he saw a "thing [that] was revealed unto [him]" but the "time appointed was long" (Dan. 10:1, KJV). Daniel initiated a twenty-one-day fast to receive more insight on the prophetic vision he had seen, which is recorded in chapter 8 (concerning the Tribulation). An angel of God (Gabriel; see Daniel 8:16; 9:21) stood before Daniel and began revealing the most detailed order of future events from Daniel's time in Babylon to the end of the Great Tribulation. (See Daniel chapters 10–12.)

Joseph's dream appeared somewhat contradictory since his mother had died in childbirth. If the moon was a symbol of Rachel and the dream alluded to Jacob and his sons ending up in Egypt, where Joseph would be second in command, then the moon should not have even been in Joseph's dream. However, consider this. The *sun* and all of the *stars* are always visible throughout the year. However, the moon is only full several days out of each month, and there is a brief period when the moon is called a *new moon*, meaning it cannot be seen in the sky from the earth. Darkness appears to fill the night, but the moon is still there nonetheless. Rachel was now dead; however, the prophet Jeremiah, hundreds of years after her death, described her weeping in her grave knowing her children would be taken captive one day:

> A voice was heard in Ramah,
> Lamentation and bitter weeping,
> Rachel weeping for her children,
> Refusing to be comforted for her children,
> Because they are no more.
>
> —JEREMIAH 31:15

How would Rachel know her children were suffering? Perhaps this is a poetic passage symbolizing the sorrow in the heart of a mother of Israel with the loss of her children. Perhaps Rachel's soul and spirit, in the netherworld of departed souls, were made aware that Israel was encountering great sorrow at the time of Jeremiah. The same would be true with the *moon* bowing before Joseph in Egypt. Benjamin, Rachel's only other son, would be present when the dream was fulfilled.

WHEN DREAMS SEEM TO CONTRADICT

This was not the only time that a prophetic vision seemed to contradict itself. In the Old Testament, two major prophets, Jeremiah and Ezekiel, predicted that the Babylonians would destroy Jerusalem in the days of King Zedekiah. Jeremiah predicted that the king of Babylon, Nebuchadnezzar, would "lead Zedekiah to Babylon" (Jer. 32:5), whereas Ezekiel predicted that "he [Zedekiah] shall not see it, though he shall die there" (Ezek. 12:13). The Jewish historian Josephus writes that since these two predictions seemed to contradict—the king would be led to Babylon and yet the king would not see it—it meant that Zedekiah rejected both predictions and refused to believe the words of either prophet.[1]

Here is how both predictions were fulfilled. In 2 Kings 25:6–7, at the final siege of Jerusalem, King Zedekiah was brought before the king of Babylon, where the Babylonians put out the king's eyes, bound him with fetters of brass, and led him into Babylon! He was *led away* but *did not see.* The king should have believed what he heard and not tried so much to figure out how it could occur.

A second example is when Isaiah told King Hezekiah that the day would come when "all that is in your house, and what your fathers have accumulated" would be carried away into Babylon, and nothing would be left (2 Kings 20:16–17). Daniel, who was a young captive in Babylon, wrote in Daniel 1:2, "Some of the articles of the house of God..." were carried to Babylon. Was it *part* or *all* of the treasures from the temple that went to Babylon? Did these two visionaries get their visions of the future crossed? Did one prophet prophesy in the *flesh* and the other in the *Spirit*? The answer lies in the text of 2 Chronicles and in Jeremiah. During the first stage of the invasion, Nebuchadnezzar took only part of the gold vessels. (See Jeremiah 27.) Nebuchadnezzar had appointed Zedekiah's brother, Jehoiakim, the new king of Judah. Jeremiah attempted to exhort Jehoiakim to submit to the Babylonian king. The Judean king refused, and thus we read: "Therefore He brought against them the king of the Chaldeans....He gave them all into his hand. And all the articles from the house of God, great and small, the treasures of the house of the LORD...all these he took to Babylon" (2 Chron. 36:17–18).

The vision was correct when the entire invasion by the Babylonians was completed.

THE AMAZING PART OF JOSEPH'S DOUBLE DREAM

As stated earlier, Joseph's mother had died in childbirth; it was impossible for her to bow with the father and the other brothers. However, notice in Joseph's sheave dream that there were eleven sheaves bowing. If we omit Joseph, there were eleven sons of Jacob who remained in the family after Joseph was sold to the traveling Ishmaelites as a slave.

Years later, when Joseph-interpreted Pharaoh's dream of a coming famine, he set aside seven years of corn to prevent Egypt from starving. When the famine struck, Joseph's brothers traveled to purchase grain in Egypt. We read where Joseph's "ten brothers went down to buy grain in Egypt" (Gen. 42:3). Benjamin was not with them; thus there were not eleven brothers as Joseph saw in his dream. When Joseph saw this, he realized this was not the complete meaning of what he had dreamed twenty-two years earlier when he saw eleven stalks of grain bowing before his sheave. He began manipulating his brothers (without their knowledge), and months later when the eleventh brother, Benjamin, arrived and all eleven bowed before Joseph, he knew this was the complete fulfillment of what he had seen in his dream. That is when he reveled himself to them! This should teach us not to try to force a dream to come to pass or to become impatient, but to exercise care and discretion when following any dream.

DREAMS—SIGNS OF A PROPHET

Prior to the completion of the Torah (first five books of the Old Testament), dreams and visions were two common methods God used to bring revelation, such as establishing covenants, warnings, and divine guidance to individuals and to the nation of Israel. The nations of antiquity, as far back as the Chaldeans in the lands of

Mesopotamia, Egypt, and Babylon, all had men in staff positions in their palaces who were considered to be dream interpreters.

Among the early Hebrews, when a man was gifted to receive dreams and visions, it was a sign that he was a prophet, or one whom God was visiting with divine insight and revelation. When King Abimelech saw Abraham's wife, Sarah, and secretly planned to take her for his wife, God appeared in a dream warning him that he would be a dead man if he so much as touched Sarah. In the dream the Almighty informed the king that Abraham was a prophet and would pray a healing prayer for Abimelech, and God would hear and answer Abraham's prayer (Gen. 20:1–7).

When Samuel was just a young child about twelve years of age, he heard the voice of the Lord calling to him on three occasions. After answering the third time, God revealed to Samuel that He was expelling the high priest Eli and his sons from the future priesthood in Israel. The vision from the Lord to Samuel came to pass. We read that "all Israel from Dan to Beersheba knew that Samuel had been established as a prophet of the LORD" (1 Sam. 3:20).

In Acts 2, on the Day of Pentecost the Holy Spirit descended upon the believers, and they were all filled with the Holy Spirit (Acts 2:1–4). Peter stood among the brethren and began expounding about the prophecies of Christ that were concealed throughout the Old Testament. Peter mentioned a prediction that David gave concerning how God would not leave the Messiah's soul in hell and not allow His holy one to see corruption (v. 31). Peter called David a prophet, since the sweet king of Israel, who had lived a thousand years before Christ, had foreseen the coming of the Messiah.

In each instance these men (and numerous others) received direct knowledge about things to come and were classified as prophets as a result of it! In the last days the Holy Spirit will speak to both young and old men. Some more liberal Christian thinkers and theologians believe that God no longer speaks today to anyone except through Scripture. The fact is, however, that God has always spoken and has never quit speaking; it's just that some people are not listening as well as others. Christ said:

> But when the Comforter is come, whom I will send unto you from the Father, even the Spirit of truth, which proceedeth from the Father, he shall testify of me.
>
> —JOHN 15:26, KJV

> However, when He, the Spirit of truth, has come, He will guide you into all truth; for He will not speak on His own authority, but whatever He hears He will speak; and He will tell you things to come.
>
> —JOHN 16:13

The Holy Spirit will speak and will show you things to come. This New Testament promise is still valid today!

three

WHY ARE SOME DREAMS DELAYED IN COMING TO PASS?

He sent a man before them—
Joseph—who was sold as a slave.
They hurt his feet with fetters,
He was laid in irons.
Until the time that his word came to pass,
The word of the LORD tested him.
The king sent and released him,
The ruler of the people let him go free.

« Psalm 105:17–20 »

When the Lord revealed to me the vision that would eventually prove to be the 9/11 attacks, about five years and three months passed before the actual event transpired. During those sixty-three months of seeing nothing that would clarify the meaning of this vision, I can remember becoming somewhat frustrated with the lack of knowing *when* this unusual vision would occur. The night vision of the tragic oil "storm" that impacted Louisiana took about thirty-three months before it was obvious that the result of the fire and collapse of the BP oil rig in the Gulf of Mexico was the clear fulfillment of the details of the night dream/vision in July of 2007.

In July of 2007, I experienced a major night vision involving an oil rig in the Gulf of Mexico. In the vision I was in the city of Baton Rouge, Louisiana, at Christian Life Fellowship with my friend, Pastor Jerry Melilli. The vision began as I was unloading our SUV at the home of a dear couple with whom we stay when we minister in the Baton Rouge area. In the vision, Pastor Melilli asked me if I had any new information or prophetic insight on what was about to occur. As if on cue, we suddenly saw a large black tornado drop from a perfectly clear sky. At that moment the scene changed, and I suddenly found myself inside the back of the *rig* (trailer) of an eighteen-wheeler truck, with one side completely open and covered with a large piece of plastic covering. There was nothing being transported in the truck. The wind struck the truck but did not harm me personally.

After exiting the truck, I heard a voice announce that another storm was forming. Again the scene changed, and I found myself in a mall; the buildings were intact, but the shoppers were missing. Lying on the mall floor were five people, both men and women, who were exposing their hands, arms, and feet and saying, "Help us. This storm has affected us. Look at our wounds." However, their wounds were *plastic* or artificial, and I knew they did not need the help and assistance that others needed. When this thought came to my mind in the vision, I heard a female voice speak and say, "Tell the churches there will be people who will claim to be in need, and they will not be—they are using the system for their benefit. Tell the churches to care for those of the household of faith first." I felt that these individuals wanted some form of money or assistance but were not actually in need as others were.

Immediately the scene changed. As I saw a second tornado was forming, I found myself in a large and rather expensive-looking restaurant filled with customers. As the storm was arriving, I ran into the men's room (a small enclosed room) to escape the violence of the wind. After the building was shaken, I returned to the main dining area, and the entire restaurant was empty. I remember thinking, "How strange for the storm not to physically affect the building, but somehow it is preventing the business from operating."

After this, I then found myself entering a small, square concrete room with a window. It was then that I was joined by two friends: Pastor Dino Rizzo, pastor of Healing Place Church in Baton Rouge, and missionary Rusty Domingue, who at the time of the vision (July 2007) was on staff at a church in Austin, Texas. However, in the vision I saw that Rusty was working with Pastor Dino. (Months later, in 2008, I was amazed when Rusty eventually moved back to Baton Rouge and began working with Dino at the Healing Place. It was just as I had seen at the time when the *storms* broke out.) Looking out the window, I saw the next tornado drop from the sky, and we all covered ourselves with a large covering to prevent any debris from falling on us. When the storm ceased, we arose safely from our secure place. Looking out of an opening in the room, I was able to see a small town's main street with little *mom-and-pop* shops that were all closed. No one was shopping in this particular area. I was again puzzled at why these tornados, which normally tear apart buildings, were not destroying buildings, only stopping people from coming into the areas for business.

Looking out the window, I saw a large fourth tornado forming in the distance. As the fourth storm formed, my entire family joined me in the room. There are several parts of the vision at this point that I have withheld from sharing in public, as they involved a national figure and his parents and some personal family members. Following this fourth storm, I was struggling to understand why these storms were occurring, how they were linked to people from Louisiana, and what the meaning was. It was the fifth and final tornado that answered my questions.

Following the fourth tornado, the scene changed from Baton Rouge to the Gulf of Mexico just off the coast of Louisiana. Pastor Dino Rizzo was standing beside me as we stared at a large oil rig in the Gulf of Mexico off the coast of Louisiana. Suddenly I saw a massive—and I do mean massive—tornado of black oil that began spinning on the gulf waters. As it spun violently, the black oil was being slung across the beautiful waters of the Gulf of Mexico. Suddenly the oil tornado struck an oil rig's platform, and I heard a strange noise, like a popping sound. The top of the tornado began to turn toward me, as though it was bowing down on the top of the water, and as it did, I heard a clicking sound. The top of the tornado became a metal cap that had bolts encircling the top of it. I yelled, "They are going to cap an oil well at an oil rig in the gulf!" I was confused as to why someone would cap a single oil well when there are hundreds of wells and rigs in the Gulf of Mexico. When I awoke, I wrote the details on a piece of paper so I would not forget what I saw. I dated it: *Thursday, July 2007, 12:30 p.m.*

Months later I called Pastor Dino, who was on a foreign trip at the time, and shared the entire incident with him. As a result, he actually made preparations in the event that a *tornado* type of storm or storms struck the area. More than a year later in the fall of 2008, Hurricane Gustav hit Baton Rouge, knocking out electricity in some areas for weeks. Dino later told me, "It happened. We were struck by this storm. Man, it was like the Tribulation down here."

I told Dino, "That is not the big one I saw in the vision. What I saw is yet to come."

Two years and nine months after the vision, on April 20, 2010, the Deepwater Horizon oil rig located in the Gulf of Mexico off the coast of Louisiana exploded. At first the explosion and its repercussions didn't *click* with me, until I began receiving numerous calls from partners of the ministry who remembered when I shared the *black oil tornado* vision with them at our Partner's Conference. When the platform collapsed and the underwater camera began to capture the oil pouring from the opening in the pipe, I was stunned—the oil looked like a miniature tornado spinning underwater! The black, unrefined oil was pouring into the waters of the Gulf of Mexico and slowly creeping toward the marshes of Louisiana.

On the forty-first day, the BP underwater camera announced that the pipe had been cut, and the camera caught a picture of the round, steel pipe with large bolts encircling it. This was where the oil was gushing into the water! I literally yelled and began calling my office workers upstairs to view the flat-screen television on the wall. "There it is," I said. "That's what I told you I saw at the top of the black oil tornado in the vision. There it is—the oil is spinning out of the top!" Then I said, "They will cap this well!"

THE MEANING OF THE FIVE STORMS

Now that I understand the meaning of the vision, why did I see four tornadoes prior to the final large one? Consider the impact of the oil on the coasts of Louisiana. There were countless trucks that delivered

Louisiana seafood to restaurants throughout the nation that were unable to deliver because of the damage to the seafood industry from the leaking oil. This resulted in thousands of personal fishing trips being canceled, which impacted the small shops in the towns along the coast that depend on those who enjoy sports fishing in the inlands and the gulf region of Louisiana to supply the shops with seafood. According to some, smaller restaurants in some towns went out of business or saw an 80 percent decline in customers during the crisis. All fishing was halted for months, and other forms of shopping in the area were also affected. Financial help was available for those whose businesses had been impacted from the crisis. However, just as in the vision, there were some individuals who sought financial assistance who didn't need direct help but were taking advantage of the situation for their personal gain. According to reports in October 2010, the fishing industry in Louisiana could suffer a loss of $115 million to $172 million as a result of the oil spill during the years of 2011 to 2013. Job losses linked to the industry number between 2,650 to 3,975, with an earnings loss of $68 to $103 million.[1] Recent reports indicate that the fishing industry in Louisiana may be impacted for several years before it fully recovers.[2]

Just as with the 9/11 vision, when a dream or vision is linked to a national warning, the understanding of the vision or dream may not always be completely understood at the time. It may take days, weeks, months, or even years before the fulfillment of the event comes to pass. However, if the dream or vision is a national warning, unless repentance can alter the outcome, the events will eventually transpire.

This was one of the challenges that even the famous Old Testament prophets had when relating prophetic warnings to their generation. Isaiah informed King Hezekiah that the Babylonians in the future would enter Jerusalem and lay siege to the city, destroying the temple and carrying the priceless gold temple treasures back to Babylon. This invasion would be restrained in the king's lifetime, but the descendants from Hezekiah's own bloodline would suffer when the moment came (2 Kings 20:16–21). The prophecy did come to pass, however, many years after Isaiah spoke it. Both Isaiah and Hezekiah were dead by then.

The prophet Jeremiah began to bring warnings of Jerusalem's coming destruction to the elders and priests at the temple in Jerusalem. He was predicting massive destruction by the Babylonians, and he even nailed the exact number of years—seventy—that the Jews would be taken captive into Babylon (Jer. 25:11–12). The priests and religious seers at the temple became so angry at Jeremiah's prophetic vision that they rose up against him and threatened to kill him for his negative warnings. In fact, Pashhur, a man who was the son of the priest and chief governor over the temple, locked Jeremiah in stocks in a dungeon to silence him (Jer. 20:1–3). Jeremiah became so discouraged at the temple leaders' and priests' unbelief and lack of concern for the danger and trouble that was coming that he determined not to speak anymore. However, when he tried to remain silent, he said it was like a "fire shut up in his bones."

> Then I said, "I will not make mention of Him,
> Nor speak anymore in His name."
> But His word was in my heart like a burning fire
> Shut up in my bones;
> I was weary of holding it back,
> And I could not.
>
> —JEREMIAH 20:9

Jeremiah was so certain his predictions were true that he purchased the field of his uncle's son for seventeen shekels of silver and took both a sealed and opened title deed, burying them in the ground in a clay (earthen) jar as a sign that the Jews would one day return to the land and rebuild on the property that would lay dormant during the captivity. (See Jeremiah 32.) The assault by the Babylonians did occur years later, as predicted, and Jeremiah chapters 51 and 52 give a detailed summary of all of the vessels and sacred pieces of furniture carried away to ancient Babylon, the city on the Tigris. The priests didn't believe Jeremiah's prediction, but the old prophet believed the word the Lord had given him.

Imagine the stress these godly men experienced in their day when warning dreams and visions from the God of Israel, Jerusalem, and the Jews came to them, and they were commissioned by God to speak aloud what was being revealed in their prayer closets. Many times their dreams and visions would not come to pass in their own lifetimes. For example, both Daniel and John saw the final prophetic empire identified as a beast with ten horns, and these predictions, which will unfold in the last day, have not yet occurred. God instructed Daniel to "seal the book until the time of the end" (Dan. 12:4), knowing these latter-day visions were a long way off. Some warnings are so advanced in their visual presentation that their fulfillment may not occur during the lifetime of the visionary. This is also true with warnings and even dreams or visions that reveal good things to come, such as the future binding of Satan, Christ's one-thousand-year reign on Earth, and the New Jerusalem coming down to Earth as seen in John's vision in the Apocalypse (Rev. 21; 22).

We also may experience a unique or encouraging dream, and we may anticipate that it should come to pass immediately. However, the Lord revealed to Abraham at age seventy-five that he would be a father of a nation (Gen. 12:1–4), but the promised son was not born until Abraham was one hundred (Gen. 17:1; 17:21). It took twenty-five years for the promise to occur. When Abraham was about eighty-five, his wife, Sarah, offered her handmaid, Hagar, to Abraham as a second wife to give a child to Abraham (Gen. 16:1–4). After ten years of waiting, Sarah knew she was barren and was attempting to *help God* fulfill her husband's promise of a son. The reason God waited until Sarah was ninety to allow her to become pregnant with Isaac is because by age ninety, Sarah had "passed the age of child-bearing" (Gen. 18:11), meaning she went through menopause, making it impossible for her to conceive. The birth of Isaac, when Abraham was one hundred and Sarah was ninety, made Isaac's conception and birth a miracle.

Joseph was seventeen when he was sold as a slave (Gen. 37:2) and thirty years old when he left a prison and became second in command over Egyptian affairs (Gen. 41:46). He had seven years to prepare for the famine (v. 53) and was two years into the famine (Gen. 45:6) when he revealed himself to his eleven brothers. Thus, twenty-two years had passed before both of Joseph's dreams were fulfilled! The entire episode was a test of God's Word in Joseph's life (Ps. 105:16–21).

In a dream of a ladder stretching upward with angels ascending and descending, Jacob was promised that he too would be blessed and would inherit the land of Abraham. After Jacob deceived his brother, Esau, his mother ordered him to get out of town and head to her brother's estate in Syria. When Rebekah sent him to Syria, she thought Jacob would just be there a "few days," until Esau cooled off (Gen. 27:44). However, Jacob spent twenty years at his uncle Laban's ranch in Syria. God eventually appeared to Jacob in a dream and instructed him to return to the Promised Land (Gen. 31:11–18). Jacob's early life was directed by dreams, but there was, and always is, a time element involved in waiting for any dream to come to pass.

I have learned by experience that an encouraging dream that reveals God's will or purpose for you may take years to come to pass, but it is given to you in advance to *undergird your faith*, helping you to continue holding on to God's promise for you. In 1988 I had a very clear dream of seeing a beautiful little girl with straight hair that appeared to be about five years of age. She was full of personality and very animated when she spoke. I asked her, "Whose little girl are you?"

She replied, "My name is Amanda, and I am the little girl you are going to have!" This little girl appeared to me in two different dreams months apart! We found out a short time later that my wife was pregnant. We both assumed the child she was carrying was a girl because of the dream. We talked about painting the baby's room pink, and our closest friends began purchasing frilly little dresses for the baby to wear. On December 23, 1989, at six o'clock in the morning, my wife gave birth to a wonderful son we named Jonathan Gabriel Stone. I was very happy since there is a blessing upon a mother when her firstborn is a male child (Exod. 13:2–15). For years we didn't think any more about the dream as we were enjoying our son so much, and he was such a trooper in traveling. After Jonathan grew up, Pam and I discussed having another child, but our travel schedule, the homeschooling of Jonathan, and other responsibilities were very time consuming.

In the year 2000, I returned home from a foreign trip. I was lying on our bed in the upstairs master bedroom, my eyes closed and very tired, when I literally felt what was the *invisible* hand of a child on my left ankle. I was so startled by it I sat up. Pam entered the room at the same time, and I told her what had happened. She asked, "What does it mean?"

I said, "I sense we are supposed to have another child!" That same year Pam became pregnant, but in the month of October, while attending our main Fall Conference, she had a miscarriage at seven weeks. After this tragedy, she felt she could not emotionally or physically carry another child. We began praying, and she became pregnant in December. I told her, "You will carry this baby, and it is the little girl I saw in the dream in 1988!"

Months later, by ultrasound, the child was confirmed to be a girl! However, in the seventh month, the OB-GYN saw an ultrasound and said to Pam, "Your embryonic fluid is low, and it is possible your child will have Down syndrome."

Pam returned home somewhat troubled. I encouraged her, "I saw a very healthy girl in that dream, and this child will NOT be sick and will NOT have an infirmity in the name of the Lord!" My wife followed the doctor's orders and went on bed rest for an entire month. At eight months into the pregnancy, on August 2, 2001, the little girl I saw *thirteen years before* in the dream was born. We named her Amanda, as this was the name she gave me in the dream. She is full of personality and is exactly like the girl in the dream. While we didn't discuss it much, during those years the dream was always in the back of my mind. Perhaps this is why it is written:

> Then the LORD answered me and said:
>
> "Write the vision
> And make it plain on tablets,
> That he may run who reads it.
> For the vision is yet for an appointed time;
> But at the end it will speak, and it will not lie.
> Though it tarries, wait for it;
> Because it will surely come,
> It will not tarry."
>
> —HABAKKUK 2:2–3

An hour after Amanda's birth I wrote this poem for her:

> Deep in sleep in the middle of the night
> A vision, a dream, such a wonderful sight

A dark-haired girl who calls me Dad
I awoke—just a dream—oh, so sad.

Days turn to years, then again you appear
Late in the night, in a dream you are there
Your name is Amanda, meaning worthy of love
I awoke and prayed to the Lord up above

That in His time make this dream come true.
Years passed, we waited for the time we'd see you.
A hand on my ankle—what is this strange sign?
An inner voice tells me, "Now is the time."

Late in October sudden tears fill our eyes
But the winter soon passes and our spirits now rise
A heartbeat is heard and an image is seen
It's a girl in the womb, "It's Amanda," we sing.

August the second, excited we wait
The time soon arrived, but the labor was great
But pain turned to joy when we all saw your face
Dark hair, it is you, in pink ribbons and lace.

Your mommy and brother and I are here
To love and protect you from danger and fear
To teach you about the place you came from
Heaven, the angels, and the land from above.

Watching you grow will be my life's joy
Until you are married with your own girl or boy
I'll be there for you till my journey is through
And when you arrive there, I'll be waiting for you.
—Written by your daddy in your mommy's room
the day you were born, August 2, 2001

There is a difference in the vision or dream *tarrying* and you being the one doing the tarrying or delaying the dream. A *tarrying dream* is one that you do not see come to pass for an extended, rather long period of time. However, at times you can delay what God is ready to perform in your life because you are fearful of failure, short of the needed provisions to fulfill it, or uncertain of the timing. You may not always receive insight of God's purpose into the future through a night dream. Your inspired dream may manifest in a strong inward pull that you sense in your spirit to take a journey, change jobs, or make a decision that could impact you or your family for years to come. At times the only way to test a *dream* or a strong inner impulse that continually throbs in your spirit is by actually stepping out in faith.

For example, I have known of individuals who were burdened to assist the poor or minister in a foreign nation through a mission project. When they saw the suffering children and the heartbreaking poverty, their hearts would reach out, but their feet never left their hometown. A year or two would pass, and the desire to travel remained, but the excuses for not going outweighed the obedience of going. There was not enough time, not enough money, and not an open door. However, *the only way to soothe the throb is to do the job* and take a journey, even if it is only one week out of a year, and minister to those faces you continually see in your *dream imagination.*

GOD GIVES YOU THE DESIRES

> Delight yourself also in the LORD, and He shall give you
> the desires of your heart.
>
> —PSALM 37:4

This word *delight* in Hebrew can allude to being *pliable,* or to enjoying something. When we begin to enjoy our relationship with God, He will give us the desires of our hearts. There are two ways this passage can be understood. The primary meaning is the word *desires,* which in Hebrew simply means "the request or the petition of our hearts." The simple meaning is that our prayers and petitions will be answered. A second, implied meaning is that God gives us our desires—in the manner of what we feel and sense in our heart and spirit was put there by the Lord.

In 1980, when I was ministering in a four-week revival in Northport, Alabama, I saw a beautiful seventeen-year-old girl named Pam standing in a group of about eighty youth who were worshiping as the choir was singing. I can still see her in my mind. I heard an inner voice say, "That is the girl you will marry." At first I tried to ignore the voice, as this was in the middle of a church service! However, the voice repeated the words twice. At that very moment she was placed in my heart—and I hadn't taken her on the first date! *She was God's desire for me, and He placed inside of me His desire.* However, His desire became my desire. We would say, "She was God's will for my life," but the will of God can only be revealed through desire. The desire I am speaking of is the other common Hebrew word for desire, *ta'avah,* meaning "to long for or delight in something." This word is found in the following passages:

> The fear of the wicked, it shall come upon him: but the desire of the righteous shall be granted.
>
> —Proverbs 10:24, kjv

> The desire of the righteous is only good: but the expectation of the wicked is wrath.
>
> —Proverbs 11:23, kjv

Hope deferred maketh the heart sick: but when the desire cometh, it is a tree of life.

—PROVERBS 13:12, KJV

The desire accomplished is sweet to the soul: but it is abomination to fools to depart from evil.

—PROVERBS 13:19, KJV

A positive dream or vision can actually motivate and stir up the desire to see the thing come to pass. It may, however, require a season of patience and careful guarding of our hearts to prevent the dream from dying within us. If you think about it, the one place where more dreams have died is at the local cemetery. So many individuals have passed on having never fulfilled those desires that were forged in their minds or birthed in their spirits. Perhaps they said, "Maybe one day when I get more time," or "When I get the money," or "When the door opens," yet they never pursued their desires.

A DELAY IS NOT A DEFEAT

Never read a delay as a defeat, just as you should never think that because you have prayed and the Lord has not answered that He is giving you a final no. The *no* may be a temporary no and not a permanent no. When Moses cried out for God to heal Miriam of leprosy, the Lord immediately said no—not at that moment, but she was healed seven days later in order to follow a pattern of the law and teach the outspoken sister of the prophet Moses to henceforth restrain herself from making careless comments. (See Numbers 12.)

Some delays are actually seasons of preparation to get the junk out of us so the Lord can get His direction in us! We are not always ready to enact God's will when we think we are. One of the greatest dangers in ministry is when a minister or even a church thinks they have *arrived* and have all of the answers. As long as the fruit on a tree is green, it will grow, but if it keeps hanging on after it matures, it can eventually turn rotten. If we maintain a teachable spirit in the process of moving toward the favor of God, we will always learn and step up to the next level of revelation for God's kingdom. Once we think that we have arrived, we can stagnate.

When Bathsheba and David's illegitimate son was born, he was stricken with a sickness. David spent seven days with his face on the ground in intercession asking God to heal the child. After seven days the child passed away. God did not heal the child, but that's not the end of the story. Bathsheba became pregnant with a second son of David's, who was named *Solomon*, meaning "peaceful" and "loved of the Lord" (2 Sam. 12:24). The sorrow of one son's early death was replaced by the joy of another son's birth. Solomon would become one of the Bible's wisest men and the builder of the most magnificent temple in Israel's history!

Not every road is straight. There will be potholes, roadblocks, and detours on the journey. This is because you must deal with people when you pursue your dream. Always remember that people will never understand what you are sensing in the same way that you do. When our ministry began to grow and I hired many wonderful workers, it took years for me to realize that they will not have the burden for the *baby* (ministry) that I birthed and carried in just the same way I will. A babysitter may love the infant he or she is watching, but once the sitter walks out the door, his or her burden and sense of responsibility is over—until the next time that sitter enters the child's home.

As a young teenage minister, I attended ministers' meetings with many wonderful pastors and evangelists of the same denomination. Many times I was returning from an extended revival—four to eleven weeks in one church, where hundreds were converted to Christ. I entered the room like a little whirlwind, excited about the

Lord's blessing and the spiritual results. Imagine one revival going eleven weeks with more than five hundred converts to Christ! Most of the time I couldn't refrain from telling what happened, and all I would get in response was a smile and a look like, "OK, let's talk about something else." It seemed the other brethren were not as excited—in reality they weren't. They would have been more thrilled if the revival had been in their church and not someone else's!

IT WILL HAPPEN QUICKLY

Most scholars believe that the famed vision in the Book of Revelation was penned about A.D. 95. For those who believe that chapters 4–22 are futuristic in their interpretation, imagine writing about the future, and more than nineteen hundred years have passed and the events still have not unfolded! This may be one reason why some suggest that the book has been fulfilled throughout history, which is called the *historic interpretation*. Within the Book of Revelation there are several revealing passages that indicate when the time will arrive for the fulfillment of the prophecies.

They shall come to pass very quickly:

> The Revelation of Jesus Christ, which God gave him to show His servants—things which must shortly take place.
> —REVELATION 1:1

> "These words are faithful and true." And the Lord God of the holy prophets sent His angel to show His servants the things which must shortly take place.
> —REVELATION 22:6

In both verses the word "shortly" does not mean it will occur in the very near future (or shortly after John's death). Both Greek words mean "rapidly, quickly and swiftly." Christ was indicating that when the time comes, these events will begin happening in succession very quickly, one after the other.

A delay in a dream or vision will cause a person to exercise patience in waiting for the event to occur. In the Bible, faith and patience are the two power twins that keep a believer from becoming weary and faint in his or her spirit while anticipating the prayer to be answered or the event to come to pass. As it is written:

> And we desire that each one of you show the same diligence to the full assurance of hope until the end, that you do not become sluggish, but imitate those who through faith and patience inherit the promises.
>
> —HEBREWS 6:11–12

> Therefore do not cast away your confidence, which has great reward. For you have need of endurance, so that after you have done the will of God, you may receive the promise.
>
> —HEBREWS 10:35–36

Remember, a delay is not a defeat. Being patient (having long endurance) is a part of the faith walk. In the end, what God has revealed will come to pass, and usually it happens very quickly.

NIGHTMARES AND DIRTY DREAMING

*When I say, "My bed will comfort me, my couch will
ease my complaint," then You scare me with dreams
and terrify me with visions.*

« Job 7:13–14 »

Many years ago in the days of cassette tapes, I taught a two-tape series simply called, "The Lust of the Flesh." My wife would tell me, "When people are at the resource table, looking over the cassette tape albums, you should see how they react to that album. When purchasing it, they turn it over so no one can see the title! It's like they are embarrassed for someone near them to think, 'Wow, are they having trouble with the lust of the flesh?'" The same is true when it comes to nightmares and dirty dreams. A person may tell you about a nightmare or a dream with frightening imagery, but there are some types of dreams no one wants to talk about. People need instruction about that, something I call *dirty dreaming.*

At times a person will experience dreams that would be considered *vile* or *violent.* In a dream a person may see a violent attacker, a thief, or a dangerous character who is attempting to harm him or a family member. These negative nightly apparitions have that individual participating in them like an actor on a stage, causing his blood pressure to rise and heart rate to increase while he is sleeping. Some people awaken and are breathing heavy. Such a dream is often called a *nightmare,* although the word has nothing to do with a female horse called a *mare.* It is said to have originated in the 1300s as *nigt-mare,* a female spirit that attempted to afflict a sleeper with the feeling of suffocating at night. The word was also used throughout parts of Europe and was eventually linked with an *incubus spirit,* which caused people to have bad dreams. By the year 1829, it became a common word to describe a bad dream.[1]

There are also rare occasions in the life of a believer when a person experiences a dream that he or she prefers not to talk about because the scenes in the dream were very lewd, vile, or seductive. It may involve the dreamer in an act of adultery, in a compromising position, or acting in a manner that the believer would never participate in. These troubling, unclean dreams can simply be called *dirty dreams.*

From a Jewish rabbinical point of view, nightmares and unclean dreams can be the result of a demonic spirit (called a *lilin* or a night spirit) that is in the room of the person attempting to sleep or in the process of sleep.[2] In the New Testament there are several terms used for wicked spirits, including: evil spirits (Luke 8:2), foul spirits (Mark 9:25, KJV), unclean spirits (Mark 1:27), spirits of infirmity (Luke 13:11), and seducing spirits (1 Tim. 4:1, KJV). These spirits are types of what Christians call demons. The word *demon* is the Greek word *daimon,* meaning "a spirit or something with divine power." In the New Testament, such as in Matthew 8:31 (KJV), the word "devils" is the Greek word *daimon.* In the Old Testament, demons were associated with idolatry and led people into worshiping idols, as indicated in Deuteronomy 32:17; Isaiah 13:21; 34:14; 65:3.[3] If an evil spirit in the atmosphere can send fiery darts (Eph. 6:16) into the mind of a believer sleeping at night, then it is no fault of a believer if they dream some strange and bizarre dream. For many years I have said that believers are certainly responsible when they are awake for what they see and hear, but they actually have no control over their sleep and any dream they may have.

Normally, if a person does not watch violent or vile movies before going to bed and has not eaten a huge meal that is causing the body to work hard to digest while the person is sleeping, he or she normally will have a regular cycle of dreams and sleep quite well. In this setting, it will be rare to have a nightmare or a dirty dream. However, there are times when you have kept your mind clean and you still have a very nasty dream. While this may happen rarely, it causes a person to feel unclean when he or she awakes. The images of the nightmare or seductive dream will remain with that person throughout the day. This is one reason why praying before going to bed and after rising up is very important. In the time of the temples, the Lord instructed the priest to place a lamb on the altar in the morning and in the evening (Exod. 29:39–42). In the morning you begin your workday, and in the evening you are preparing to rest. Prayer can renew your mind in the morning when you begin your day and in the evening as you conclude your day. We no longer apply the physical blood of a slain animal, but through our faith and confession we can apply the blood of Christ, the Lamb of God, and this is how believers overcome Satan (Rev. 12:11).

THE SOURCE OF NIGHTMARES

There is no direct Scripture passage or, to my knowledge, church tradition as to why at times sweet dreams turn sour. After many years of a full-time traveling ministry, I have several suggestions from the library of personal experience.

The atmosphere surrounding you

If you travel much, you soon learn that all hotels and motels have their own *atmosphere*. The *spiritual air* has little or nothing to do with the type of bed, the colors in the room, or the pictures on the wall. Early in my ministry, our local church revivals would often continue for an average of two weeks, some lasting as long as eleven weeks each night—without a break. Pam and I, and later Jonathan, our son, would live in a small motel room with a bed, a round table, and two chairs for weeks on end. In the early days, few churches could afford to provide a suite or a large living space, and the smaller towns did not have contemporary facilities. Believe me, after about two weeks, *cabin fever* hit us, and we had to get out for brief periods to prevent the four walls from driving us a little batty! I recall in the early 1980s that there was one hotel in Calhoun, Georgia, where we camped out in one small room for three weeks. My wife and I experienced extreme difficulty sleeping, were restless the entire time, and felt uneasiness with the entire place. It took me several years to realize that in a motel/hotel setting, there were other people sleeping in the room before we arrived who may have had their own unclean spirits controlling their lives, and individuals possessed with unclean spirits may be sleeping in a room next door!

These individuals are often not Christians and may spend their evening watching pornography, violence, or horror movies on the hotel cable or pay channels. At times, some folks would be in their rooms high on drugs, and you could occasionally hear men through the walls mumbling in a loud tone under the influence of alcohol. The lesser-priced hotel rooms attracted more of these types of individuals. We have actually heard couples fighting behind closed doors or groups of young people partying in their rooms until three in the morning, knowing we had to be up at seven for an early Sunday morning service at the church. There were times I felt like getting up, opening the door, and just yelling, "Praise God," at the top of my lungs in retaliation to the beer guzzlers who disrupted my sleep all night!

The atmosphere in the more family-oriented hotel chains did not permit these types of disruptions, and thus sleep came easier and naturally. After years of pondering why some rooms seemed more restful than others, I realized that when a person sleeps (in a room near me), if that person is under the influence of an unclean spirit, that spirit does not sleep when the person is sleeping, because the spirit world does not require sleep as we humans do (Ps. 121:4). Thus when a person is sleeping, the evil spirit is free to enter and exit the person's body at will (Matt. 12:43). At times I could sense a troubling presence in my room and knew it was not something I had invited to join me!

An example in the Bible is when King Saul was troubled by an evil spirit, and as David played the harp, the evil spirit departed from Saul, and he was "refreshed and well" (1 Sam. 16:23). At a later time, the same spirit returned to Saul, and he attempted to kill David with a javelin (1 Sam. 18:10–11). Only when David ministered to Saul through anointed music was the nervous king relieved from his mental oppression. Just as this evil spirit could enter and exit at times, when Pam and I would stay in certain areas, our sleep could be disrupted, I believe, by evil entities that were roaming in the night. This uneasy presence in the atmosphere may be the result of who was previously in the room or who is staying in nearby rooms.

The spirits ruling over the region

During our extensive evangelistic traveling ministry, there were two major cities in which I could sense a very dark, almost depressing or oppressive spiritual presence. The first was Savannah, Georgia, and the other was Tampa, Florida. My first experience in Savannah was shortly after I was married in the early 1980s. We were staying in the home of the pastor of a large church where I was ministering nightly. Both my wife and I were very restless and unable to get any complete sleep. Our dreams were very troubling and left us tired when we arose. After extended prayer I sensed there was some form of *occult spirit* in the area. When I told the pastor, he revealed this to the church, as Reverend Lester Sumrall had recently stated that he sensed a very strong occult spirit over the city. The pastor stood before the church and said that it was confirmed that there was a spirit of the occult over the area. That night we also learned of a group of six witches who lived across the street from the pastor's house. Thus our own spirits were sensitive to the very atmosphere in the area.

In the late 1980s we began ministering in the Tampa area. The area we were ministering in and staying in was located in South Tampa. At the time this was perhaps the darkest and most oppressive atmosphere I had ever encountered. Our son was still an infant, and each night at exactly twelve thirty he would awake, screaming and shaking. This went on the entire time we were in the city and ceased when we departed. I soon discovered that the Tampa area was noted for being a very seductive area, with one man in particular in charge of numerous adult strip clubs and other forms of pornography that surrounded us in every direction. It was a city where certain types of people came out at night to party, drink, take drugs, and pack out the strip clubs. It was also rumored that the Mafia had moved their center to Tampa because of the drugs being run through Florida.

It appears that often the atmosphere in major cities can be traced to the types of sins, iniquities, and carnal pleasures that dominate or control those living in those particular areas. Sin is more than a three-letter word. It involves carnal thoughts that lead to actions that impact the person and alter the person's personality, which in return alters the spiritual atmosphere. When there are numerous believers influencing the morals and laws of a community, there will follow a spirit of peace and tranquility throughout the region. When drugs are being sold on street corners, gangs roam like hungry wolves, bars are filled with drunken men, and seducing spirits capture the imagination of the youth, then a covering of spiritual evil can be felt when a person is awake and asleep. As it is written, "When the righteous are in authority, the people rejoice; but when a wicked man rules, the people groan" (Prov. 29:2).

The signs and sounds stuck in your head

The third possible reason for the type of dream is related to what a person may see or hear prior to going to bed. Years ago in Ohio, I was concluding a message when a man jumped to his feet shouting, "My boy…please help my boy; something is wrong with him!" I asked the church to stretch their hand toward the lad, who appeared to be having a seizure. We began to pray, and I did as Christ would—I began rebuking the spirit that was attacking the eleven-year-old. Immediately the shaking stopped and his eyes were back to normal. The father was weeping and the church rejoicing.

Afterward I asked the father if his son was an epileptic, and he responded, "No." He then said, "This has never happened before." I was in shock and could not understand why this had happened to the lad. Then the father confessed, "I allowed him to watch the movie *The Exorcist* on a movie channel. Do you think this opened a door?"

My jaw dropped, and I just stared at him for a moment. I knew the Bible told of a young child that a spirit had controlled, often throwing him into the water and fire to destroy him (Mark 9:20– 23). I also recalled where the father informed Christ that a spirit had come upon his son from the time he had been a child (v. 21). Spirits can physically attack children, but it is important not to allow any form of visual or verbal activities that emphasize the occult, demonic activity, or seductive sexual innuendos from planting seeds in their minds. Such seed planted can actually open a door to a tormenting or oppressive spirit. It may have been fear of what the lad saw that opened the door for a physical attack to come.

If you enjoy bloodthirsty horror movies with vampires chewing human flesh and coloring their fangs with human blood, then never question why you are having terrible dreams at night. If you spend your free time feeding your spirit violent programs, movies, or reading the latest "kill them and bury them" magazines, then when you begin dreaming that you are carrying a shotgun shooting up the innocents in the town, you have sights and sounds stuck in your head during the day whose wrong *seeds* are producing bad *fruit* in the night.

Many men are drawn to a secret addiction—Internet pornography. In the past, full nudity was only available to purchase under the counter at certain stores or purchased as pay-per-view movies. The technology has now moved to the personal laptop, with thousands of images available with the click of the button. The male mind can be easily pulled into the cyber world of pornography, cementing images on the brain that will never be removed. Men will then go to bed with their wives, uninterested in her love and affection, having become rooted in an emotional affair with a lifeless, full-color image of a female stranger. Peaceful sleep will turn into a tormenting nightmare or a *dirty dream*, which will leave even a loving husband restless in the morning from a night journey in the world of the subconscious. Many homes are being wrecked because a man or woman became connected to a total stranger on the World Wide Web. Perhaps the word *web* describes well what can happen when you log on to the wrong sites.

HOW TO STOP NIGHTMARES AND DIRTY DREAMING

Set the atmosphere in the room.

I have discovered by experience some practical insights on how you can change the atmosphere. Years ago a Christian musician, Phil Driscoll, shared how music alters any atmosphere. He told that when he checked into a hotel, he took a tape player with praise and worship cassettes. When he went out for a meal, he left the music playing to *purge the atmosphere* in the room. After hearing this, I decided to try this, and did—and it became a routine, not just on one occasion, but continually during my extended revivals. The Word and worship coming from the cassette tapes (now CDs) filled the atmosphere. When I would forget the tapes, I would keep the television channel on a Christian television program.

You can experience this *shifting* in a church service. The atmosphere begins to change, similar to when clouds bring a cool rain in the summer heat. The Bible is God's written Word, but it must be spoken to become a life-changing force. There is no difference between someone speaking (or singing) in person and speaking or singing on a DVD or audio CD, as there is power and authority in the spoken Word (Heb. 4:12).

Set the atmosphere in the room where you are going to sleep, including your own personal bedroom. If it is not with worship music, then let it be through prayer and personal worship prior to sleeping. Worship brings heaven down to the earth, and evil spirits are unable to remain in the same room where the worshipers are exalting Christ. In Mark 5 there was one man possessed by a legion of evil spirits. However, when Christ stepped off the boat, the possessed man "ran and worshiped him" (Mark 5:6). Not even a legion of spirits could prevent this man from worshiping the Lord!

Purge the mind by the renewal of the spirit.

There is a simple but powerful passage in 2 Corinthians 4:16: "Therefore we do not lose heart. Even though our outward man is perishing, yet the inward man is being renewed day by day." The same thought is repeated in Colossians 3:10: "...and have put on the new man who is renewed in knowledge according to the image of Him who created him." The Greek word for *renewed* in these passages comes from two words: *ana*, meaning "back again," and *kainos*, meaning "made different." It means to make different again.[4] It is a continual process of making it new and helping you to think differently. The renewing of the mind is a daily process. Throughout a common day, there is much clutter and excessive baggage that distracts and fills our thoughts. To remove this means to clear the channels through the "washing of water by the word" (Eph. 5:26).

I have never been able to explain this, but every time I have opened my Bible and began to read it, there is a peace and a renewal that I sense. There are wisdom books such as Psalms and Proverbs that give practical instructions and inspire a person's spirit. After reading and meditating on the Scriptures, my mind feels clean and refreshed. It can be compared to the mind being washed in water!

Claim the promises of rest.

There are two beautiful passages believers can read, speak aloud, and receive for their personal benefit prior to going to bed at night:

> I will both lie down in peace, and sleep; for You alone, O LORD, make me dwell in safety.
>
> —PSALM 4:8

> When you lie down, you will not be afraid; yes, you will lie down and your sleep will be sweet.
>
> —PROVERBS 3:24

One of my staff workers, Andrea Anderson, shared during a Friday morning staff devotional how when she was a little girl she would have nightmares continually. Her father, a dedicated believer, would go into her room and pray for her to have a good night's sleep. She commented, "Every time my dad prayed, I would go right to sleep and never have a scary dream or nightmare. However, if for some reason he was not able to pray, it seemed on those nights I did not sleep as well and would have disturbing dreams."

Having two children, my wife and I have both discovered the significance of praying with our children prior to their going to sleep each night. We have taught our children never to go to sleep without first praying. Our daughter is read a story each night, and she prays a special prayer from her heart. She sleeps very well and always gets up alert and ready to go. (I wish I could bottle that energy!) I can recall our son, Jonathan, as a young child lying beside me in the bed, and we would talk about how there were angels assigned to protect children. At times, just before he went to sleep he would say, "Dad, raise your hands and see if you can feel an angel in the room!" He nicknamed my right arm the "angel detector"! We had so much fun, and he too rested well and seldom (that I can recall) awoke with any form of troubling dream.

During Christ's earthly ministry, parents would present their children to Christ requesting Him to lay His hands upon them and bless them. In my book *Breaking the Jewish Code,* under the chapter that deals with how Jewish parents raise their children according to life cycles, I wrote about the importance of parents blessing their children:

> The Torah reveals the importance of verbally blessing your children. Isaac spoke blessings over Jacob and Esau (Gen. 27), and Jacob blessed the two sons of Joseph (Gen. 48), later passing blessings to his sons (Gen. 49). Before Moses's death, he pronounced a prophetic blessing on the tribes of Israel (Deut. 33). Devout Jewish parents and grandparents continually offer blessings over their children and grandchildren, believing in God's ability to transfer His favor through their prayers.
>
> Blessings are preformed on Sabbath days, feast days, and various special occasions. It is important to begin the prayers of blessing when the children are young, tenderhearted, and more receptive, as they tend to feel more awkward as they enter their late teens.
>
> The pattern for blessing children is narrated in Genesis 48:2, when Jacob blessed Ephraim and Manasseh. Jacob sat on the edge of his bed when blessing his grandsons. The writer to the Hebrews wrote that Jacob blessed his own sons, "…leaning on the top of his staff" (Heb. 11:21). Today, those performing the blessing on their children prefer to stand up in respect to approaching God's throne. When preparing for a blessing, ask the children to bow their heads, teaching them reverence to God, and tell them the blessing was practiced by their ancestors

as in Genesis 24:48 and in Exodus 12:17, when Israel was departing from Egypt.

In Hebrew, the word *smicha* means, "laying on of hands." In the temple, the priest would lay hands upon animals, symbolizing the transfer of sins. On the Day of Atonement, a goat was used, which became the scapegoat. Jacob blessed the sons of Joseph, Ephraim and Manasseh by laying hands upon their heads (Gen. 48:14). Before his death, Moses transferred his wisdom and authority to Joshua by the laying on of hands (Deut. 34:9).

Prior to the blessing, lay both hands upon the head of the child or one hand on the head of each child if there are two children. A general Jewish blessing that is prayed every Sabbath by the father over his a son is: "May God make you as Ephraim and Manasseh." A general blessing spoken over a daughter is: "May God make you as Sarah, Leah, Rebekah, and Rachel." A favorite blessing that can be pronounced is the same words Jacob spoke over Ephraim and Manasseh:

The Angel who has redeemed me from all evil,
Bless the lads;
Let my name be named upon them,
And the name of my fathers Abraham and Isaac;
And let them grow into a multitude in the midst of the
　　earth.

—GENESIS 48:16

One ancient blessing that was prayed over the people by the high priest is the special blessing the priest prayed over the people in the time of Moses and at both Jewish temples.

The LORD bless you and keep you;
The LORD make His face shine up you,

And be gracious to you;
The LORD lift up His countenance upon you,
And give you peace.

—NUMBERS 6:24–26[5]

Another important comment from the book reads:

Christ's disciples said, "Teach us how to pray" (Luke 11:1). They knew Christ engaged in early morning prayer (Mark 1:35) and witnessed miracles resulting from His prayer life. The best way of teaching your children how to pray is to be an example and pray yourself!

As a child in the 1960s, I can recall my father praying in his upstairs church office with the windows opened. I just knew they could hear him across the river at the county jail. Many times in the evening I could hear Dad's prayers filtering up through the air vents in my bedroom floor as he interceded in the basement of our house. When I was sick or in difficulty, I believed God would hear Dad's prayers. His prayer life was an example and a pattern for me to understand *how* to pray. Let your children see and hear you pray at home, and not just in church.

The simplest *beginner* prayers are praying at bedtime. In bedtime prayer, Orthodox Jews mention four archangels, two which are mentioned in the Bible (Michael and Gabriel) and two found in Apocryphal (nonbiblical) sources. They pray, "In the name of the Lord, the God of Israel: Michael on my right, Gabriel on my left, Uriel before me, Raphael behind me, and above my head the Shekinah [presence] of God." Raphael was traditionally an angel of healing, and Uriel was believed to be the guiding light of the Holy Scriptures.[6] Children should learn a bedtime prayer as soon as they can speak.

Before sending a child off to school, a parent should

pray with them. Using the scripture "So Abraham rose early in the morning" (Gen. 22:3), the *Shacharit,* meaning "early morning hour," prayers were the first of three daily prayers. The moment a devout Jew awakes, he prays, "I gratefully thank You, O living and eternal King, for You have returned my soul within me with compassion— abundant is Your faithfulness."[7] We know Christ prayed a great while before sunrise (Mark 1:35), and at the temple morning prayers were offered as the sun rose, beginning a new day. As a parent, speak a protective prayer over your children before they depart from the security of your dwelling.[8]

Perhaps you are a single parent and are very busy working and raising your children. It is important for you to use those special moments at night prior to your child (or children) going to bed to share a devotional and for you to personally pray over your children, asking the loving heavenly Father to give them "sweet sleep" (Prov. 3:24). If you are troubled with your own ability to properly rest at night, then consider the following promise from the Word of God:

> You will keep him in perfect peace, whose mind is stayed on You, because he trusts in You.
>
> —Isaiah 26:3

> You will guard him and keep him in perfect and constant peace whose mind [both its inclination and its character] is stayed on You, because he commits himself to You, leans on You, and hopes confidently in You.
>
> —Isaiah 26:3, amp

In the 1611 King James translation the verse says "perfect peace." In Hebrew, the original language of Isaiah, it reads that God will preserve you in "shalom, shalom." The Hebrew word *shalom* means "to be at peace, to be complete and whole." It is used among Jews as a greeting similar to saying "good morning" or "hello" and is often used when saying good-bye.

If the English translators had translated this literally, it would read: "that God will guard you in 'peace, peace…'" In English the repetition of a word back to back would appear to be a grammatical error. In English you would never say, "God loves, loves you," or "You look good, good," but you would say, "God has *great* love for you," or "You look exceptionally well." It appears that when the Bible translators saw the words "peace, peace," they translated the two words for peace as "perfect peace." Years ago as I was meditating on this double peace reference, I recalled that the human brain consists of two different hemispheres, the left and right, with each hemisphere being the command center for different parts of the body. This double peace, to me, can allude to peace covering both the left and right hemisphere in the human brain! In other words, God will keep (guard) and secure all parts and sections of your mind in His peace!

God believes in rest. He set a pattern for us all when He rested on the seventh day of Creation (Gen. 2:2) and established a day of rest each week for us to enjoy (Exod. 16:26–29). He also desires that you sleep well and that your dreams be peaceful, not troubling, and that you be instructed by the Word and the Holy Spirit to discern between a carnal nightmare and a true spiritual warning from the Lord.

five

FALSE PROPHETS AND FALSE DREAMS

I have heard what the prophets have said who prophesy lies in My name, saying, "I have dreamed, I have dreamed!" How long will this be in the heart of the prophets who prophesy lies? Indeed they are prophets of the deceit of their own heart, who try to make My people forget My name by their dreams which everyone tells his neighbor, as their fathers forgot My name for Baal.

« Jeremiah 23:25–27 »

When writing about the significance of spiritual dreams, I want to be perfectly clear that a person is not to live their life by dreams but by the Word of God. A true dream or vision will always be in agreement with the written Scriptures and will complement the will of God in a person's life. The Scriptures make it clear that some self-acclaimed prophets can and will attempt to manipulate the hearts of innocent and sincere individuals with a false word and false dream.

From the time of Moses and throughout the generations of the biblical prophets, one of the major thorns in the flesh of true prophets was the number of false prophets who often challenged the prophets of the Lord. In the time of King Ahab, a battle strategy was being planned in the war room, and King Jehoshaphat had aligned himself with the wicked leader Ahab. King Ahab marched his procession of *prophetic puppets* before his throne, all of them sounding like a broken record—predicting that if Ahab would go to battle, he would win! King Jehoshaphat sensed the hollow sound of these predictions, which sounded like a parrot repeating the same words. He demanded to hear from one true prophet of the Hebrew God. The only man of God capable of bringing a true word was being held in the dungeon to prevent his *negative* predictions from mixing with the *positive* prophets and possibly confusing someone! The *real* prophet, Micaiah, was released long enough to give a word, only he was placed on a verbal restriction from the prison guard to only speak a smooth, positive word that agreed with the false prophets. He played the game, until Ahab demanded him to speak the truth.

That's when the wicked king got an earful! Micaiah saw a vision in which the angels of heaven were gathered on the left and right side of God's throne. The prophet saw where God was going to set up Ahab to be slain in the battle by permitting a "lying spirit" to deceive all of the palace's false prophets and set up Ahab to believe their lying prediction of victory (2 Chron. 18:1–27). I call this *the battle of the dueling prophets*. One alleged prophet, Zedekiah, slapped Micaiah on the face and demanded to know, "Which way did the spirit from the LORD go from me to speak to you?" (v. 23). One man was predicting a great victory and the other was predicting death. One was going to be correct and the other proven a liar. God's prophet won the duel!

PERSONAL PROPHECY

Today there is a real hunger among multitudes to experience a genuine, life-changing spiritual encounter and to hear a clear word from the Lord. Any individual who has an inner craving for knowledge, understanding, and wisdom must begin feeding himself or herself with what is called the "milk of the word" (1 Pet. 2:2). It is written in Hebrews 5:13 that those who use milk are babes in Christ and are not skilled in the word of righteousness. That is, they do not yet understand the deeper things of God. The spiritual meat (v. 14) is for the strong and mature believer. For example, a new convert to Christ should not attempt to tackle the prophetic teachings in the Book of Revelation! He or she should begin with the simple yet profound doctrines of salvation, sanctification, and the Holy Spirit baptism. Most ministers suggest that babes in Christ study the Gospel of John first. Also, new converts need knowledge in baptism in water and how to live and walk by faith. Once the foundations of faith have been laid, then a believer can move on to the deeper truths in the Scripture. The writer of Hebrews wrote:

> But solid food [meat] belongs to those who are of full age, that is, those who by reason of use have their senses exercised to discern both good and evil.
>
> —HEBREWS 5:14

As believers read, study, and feed from the Word of God, their spiritual hunger and thirst will be satisfied. The Word of God is "quick, and powerful" (Heb. 4:12, KJV). These two words mean "alive and energized." I have more than fifty thousand hours of Bible study, research, and reading of thousands of books; I have often said that some people need a drug to get them high, but my *high* comes from receiving a nugget or insight from God's Word that I was unaware of! The answers on how to believe, how to pray, how to treat others, and how to give and be a blessing are all found in the Bible. The new covenant is established on promises, and you can live a victorious life when you plant the seed of the Word in you and allow it to mature and bring forth fruit of righteousness.

Many believers, however, have never learned to hear that still small voice within and to follow those little nudges and sudden inner urges. The Holy Spirit directs and leads us from inside our spirit. Because baby believers may struggle with understanding and hunger to hear from the Lord, they can easily become caught up with a person who allegedly is giving out *personal prophecies*. A personal prophecy is usually spoken by someone who has labeled himself or herself as a *prophet* or a *prophetess*.

I am a fourth-generation minister and have a very solid heritage in the truth of the Word, and I have seen about every type of spiritual *fruit and nut* that has ever popped out of the Christian garden. I have heard from deluded individuals who claimed they were Elijah or one of the two witnesses of Revelation 11. I have read the letters of self-acclaimed prophets who said if I did not send them money, I would be under a curse. I have heard of deceivers who would manipulate the masses or use their alleged prophetic gifts to draw in income for their own selfish greed. One-self acclaimed prophet came to a church in Georgia to *preach*, claiming he was gifted with a special anointing to increase your blessing under one condition: if you gave an offering to his ministry. The only *catch* was that the length and type of prayers he was *anointed* to pray for a person were based upon the amount of money that person gave to him in the offering. The man organized four different lines: the $50, $500, $1,000, and $5,000 lines. Those giving $50 got a slap on the head and a "God bless you." The $500 folks got a longer prophecy with more *benefits* guaranteed for their obedience. The one woman who gave $5,000 received a long *word*, a long prayer, the personal address of the self-acclaimed prophet, and his private phone number.

The sad aspect is that Christians sitting under this shyster's ministry believed he had some hotline to heaven that could release God's special favor. For some reason, many of these self-acclaimed prophets and prophetesses link their ability to be a blessing to you on the amount of money that comes from you. Can you imagine the apostle Peter's reaction today if he was a false prophet and Simon the sorcerer from Samaria came to him and said, "I'll give you money, if you will give me the gift of laying hands upon people to receive the Holy Spirit"? (See Acts 8:18–19.) Some of today's so-called prophets would grab Simon, bring him to the platform, and shout, "Folks, God is moving! This man is a sorcerer, but he has felt impressed to plant a large seed in the ministry. You know God can bless a man even if he's not all right at this time, so raise your hands this way and let's pray a blessing on him!"

However, Peter was a true prophet, and instead of taking the magician's money, Peter rebuked Simon and said, "Your money perish with you, because you thought that the gift of God could be purchased with money!" (Acts 8:20). Peter discerned the sorcerer was "poisoned by bitterness and bound by iniquity" (v. 23).

While some may disagree with what I am going to say, when it comes to the area of personal prophecy, I cannot find in the Scriptures where any apostle or prophet had a ministry of continually giving individuals a *word from the Lord.* At times they received a word of wisdom or a word of knowledge (1 Cor. 12:7–10), but no believers stood in a long line to *get a word*; instead they sat and heard the preaching of God's Word and then allowed the Holy Spirit to confirm that word through signs, wonders, and the gifts of the Holy Spirit (Heb. 2:4). I once had a worker who was constantly saying, "The Lord told me this, and He told me that." The problem arose when little of what she said came to pass! I told my wife, "This girl seems to receive more words from God than the prophets of the Bible received."

Most of the personal prophetic utterances in the New Testament were words of *warning*—not *blessings* or *guarantees of prosperity.* (See Acts 11:28; 21:10–11.) In fact, in the Book of Acts, the disciples in Jerusalem were selling their property and dividing the money among other believers. The main reason was that Christ had already predicted that Jerusalem would be destroyed within one generation. If the city was doomed, then why continue living there? These followers of Christ *got out while the getting was good!* The message they heard was not, "Yea, I say I am going to bring thee out and prosper thy business with great money for the kingdom." It was, "Not one stone shall be left upon another....When you see Jerusalem surrounded by armies...flee to the mountains....Let him who is on the housetop not go down to take anything out of his house" (Matt. 24:2; Luke 21:20–21; Matt. 24:17). A real prophet would not just pronounce a prosperity blessing on the unsanctified, but he would chastise the ungodly and rebuke the believer who was living contrary to the Word of God.

I feel about this issue the way the great minister named Lester Sumrall did. I once heard him teach and say that he believed that under the new covenant, if you prayed and lived close to the Lord in the way you should, the Lord would speak directly to you, and you would not need a second party to bring the message to you! Any *word* from a second party would only confirm what you already knew in your heart. This is the reason why anyone giving a prophecy is required to be judged by others (1 Cor. 14:29). Some believers remind me, "But Paul talked about the gift of prophecy and said all could prophesy." We must understand that the word *prophesy* does not hold just one meaning—to reveal the future. Paul said that "you can all prophesy…that all may learn and all may be encouraged" (v. 31). A *prophetic word* in the church comes from a person who speaks under divine inspiration to edify, exhort, and comfort believers through the revelation of the Word and the Spirit (v. 3). A prophetic word may contain a warning of coming danger.

As believers mature in the Word and in their spiritual walk, they will discover that God begins to direct them inwardly. Then the Almighty will release words of wisdom and knowledge, and eventually He will permit insight to be revealed through dreams and visions. You must exercise discernment, however, when any individual begins to relate a dream in which *you* were in the dream. You should have knowledge of that person's spiritual life, his or her integrity in the Word, and if past dreams have had true meanings and have come to pass. Otherwise, some may either ignorantly or willingly manipulate a person's plans or decisions by a dream that is misinterpreted.

In the late 1980s I was hosting a tour to Israel with more than two hundred fifty believers joining me. A woman who was not going on the trip was washing dishes when suddenly she dropped a glass, and it broke. She said that suddenly she had a vision in her mind and heard a voice say, "Those going to Israel will come back broken like this glass!" She immediately called her friends and encouraged them to cancel their trip or they would return broken or injured. People planning to travel on the tour began calling me, concerned for their safety.

That is when I shared with them that years ago the Lord gave me a solid, faith-building word about any time I would travel to the Holy Land, saying, "The LORD your God is with you wherever you go" (Josh. 1:9). Since receiving that word in 1986, I have never hesitated to make the journey each year.

At that time, some fearful travelers canceled and others went. We returned, and no one was hurt or injured. The woman totally misread what she *felt*.

Often when a person *misses their prediction*, they will attempt to cover their mistake. This was witnessed with a man who wrote a book titled *88 Reasons Why the Rapture Will Be in 1988*. The book caught on like a brush fire, with millions of Christians waiting until that set day in September to see if indeed the day and hour had arrived. When the date passed, the author wrote a new book, stating he had missed the fact that there is no zero year between 1 B.C. and A.D. 1. Thus he suggested the calculation was off by one year. The new date was the fall of 1989. After that date passed, we never heard back from the fellow.

The false prophets of the Old Testament had no ability to "read the times" in the same manner the righteous prophets could. One tribe of Israel was given a gift of *knowing* where things were *going*:

> ...of the sons of Issachar who had understanding of the times, to know what Israel ought to do...
>
> —1 CHRONICLES 12:32

"I WILL MARRY PERRY"

Many years ago I was preaching a three-week revival in Montgomery, Alabama. At the time I was a twenty-two-year-old single preacher who was engaged to be married the following Friday after the revival closed. After I stood to announce that I was leaving Montgomery to get married in Northport, I received a call the following morning from a woman from the church. She said that she had a dream that I was missing the will of God and should not be getting married at that time. She was very adamant and said she heard from the Lord a lot, and I should take heed to her warning. Herein was the *clash* between the *dueling revelations*. This woman said she was hearing from the Lord. However, the Holy Spirit had spoken to me in a four-week revival three years earlier at the same church in Northport, Alabama, telling me that I would marry a beautiful girl named Pam Taylor. For more than two and one-half years we *dated* by phone. I was certain I was in the will of God and had perfect peace (which I discovered is the key to knowing you are in the will of God). I found out later that the woman who called had a teenage daughter who had a *crush* on me during the revival. This woman was obviously speaking out of her own spirit, since I have been happily married for more than thirty years!

The point is that when a second-party person brings you warnings, you must "recognize those who labor among you, and are over you in the Lord and admonish you" (1 Thess. 5:12) in order to determine the level of trust you can safely place in their words. Just as the Bible teaches, "Do not lay hands on anyone hastily" (1 Tim. 5:22), we must exercise caution in receiving a *personal word*. It is very possible that the Lord can and will use another person to speak a warning or an encouragement into your life, as this is one way the body of Christ can "bear one another's burdens" (Gal. 6:2). However, the *word* must be judged. I know of one man who claims a major *prophetic gift* and continually makes predictions that are all marked as a *word from the Lord*. His reputation is in doubt because of his level of *accuracy*, as more than 50 percent of the time what he predicts never happens (he often places dates and times upon events). I don't know about you, but this is not the type of person I want giving me a *word*, for how would I know if it was from the Lord or if he was just speaking out of his own intellect?

It reminds me of the story of a minister who called a woman from the audience and announced, "God said you are called to go to China." She began weeping. He called a man out and said, "The Lord says you are called to be a missionary in India." He began crying, and he grabbed the woman, and they both were arm in arm crying. The minister said, "Do you know each other?"

The woman said, "Yes, we are husband and wife!" In an attempt to get out of the dilemma, the minister cried out, "I see it now— you are both called to Indochina!" Of course he was off target, but the couple lived in fear that they were out of God's will. One of my ministry partners, who has a successful personal business, called me concerned and said, "A man came to our church who said he was a prophet. He called me up, telling me I was to prepare to travel full-time overseas, preaching and singing the gospel. First, I can't sing. Second, I don't feel called, but now I am totally confused!"

I replied, "God is not the author of confusion (1 Cor. 14:33), and if you don't bear witness with the prophetic word he gave, then pay no attention to it, as it must be judged before it is received anyway (1 Cor. 14:29). You are a praying man, and you can hear from God for yourself!" This is one reason why we are to "know them which labour among you" (1 Thess. 5:12, KJV).

The Lord instructed Moses, "It there arises among you a prophet or a dreamer of dreams, and he gives you a sign or a wonder, and the sign or the wonder comes to pass, of which he spoke to you, saying, 'Let us go after other gods'—which you have not known…you shall not listen to the words of that prophet or that dreamer of dreams" (Deut. 13:1–3). That person would be a false prophet.

JUDGING THE DREAM

It seems odd that we must *judge* a dream or vision, but this is true, since there are dreams that come from the flesh, dreams that come from the Spirit of God, and fiery mental darts (Eph. 6:16) that can create a dream from the presence of some unclean spirit, which may shoot an arrow in a believer's mind while he is asleep. How do we judge a dream?

Judge it by the Word of God.

As we have and will continue to discuss in this book, there are established methods we can use to determine if a dream is from the Lord. The greatest confirmation comes directly from the Word of God. If the dream instructs or implies that you are to act, speak, or live in a way contrary to God's Word, then it is not from the Lord. One married man said he had a dream that he was to leave his wife and marry another woman in the church, who was also married, thus breaking up two marriages to *fulfill God's purpose.* This is a seducing dream and definitely not from the Lord. According to Ephesians 5:25, husbands are to love their wives as Christ loved the church, and a "bishop then must be…the husband of one wife" (1 Tim. 3:2). If it's not right, it won't stand the test in the "light" (Ps. 119:105).

Judge it by the reputation of the dreamer.

The Bible is clear; there are occasional false teachers and false prophets. The apostle John wrote that there was a woman, identified as Jezebel, who "calls herself a prophetess" and who was sexually seducing men in the church (Rev. 2:20). She had a reputation on Earth as a prophetess, but in heaven she was a seducer. We need to begin to see people as *heaven sees* them, not as people *perceive them.* I have known of believers who truly loved God, but they followed ministries whose leaders were morally repugnant in their private lives, beating their companion, cursing, sleeping with numerous women, getting drunk, and still trying to reveal the mysteries of God in prophetic words. The reputation of the minister and the credibility of what he has spoken in the "name of the Lord" must always be considered before accepting any alleged word that God is sending you through a person.

For a moment I must boast about my precious father, who is a very humble individual. He can hardly talk about the Lord without weeping, and when he relates the old stories, he breaks down every time and cries. I cannot tell you the number of times Dad has experienced a warning dream or a vision, and it came to pass in great detail. In fact, I cannot think of one time when he was warned about something when the dream or vision did not come to pass. This is the test of a true prophetic person who is sensitive to the Holy Spirit.

One of the most bizarre accounts occurred years ago when we were praying in a house together. Dad began to "pray in the Spirit" (1 Cor. 14:15) and soon saw a mental vision. He said, "The Lord told me that great darkness is coming out of Lebanon. He also said that there would be confusion created between Yasser Arafat's group and Hamas." Within a few months Lebanon began stirring, and eventually Israel had a major summer war with Hezbollah in Lebanon. I was stunned when the PLO and Hamas in Gaza began killing each other during a power struggle. Dad used the word *Hezbos* and said the Lord would eventually judge "Hezbos."

I said, "Dad, it is Hezbollah."

He said, "I heard the word *Hezbos*."

I decided to go to the Internet and look up this word. It was actually a derogatory abbreviation and name for Hezbollah in Lebanon! The Lord was speaking down on this terror group! The word *Hezbos* is the plural form of *Hezbo*, which is often an abbreviated word for the name of the Hezbollah. In some instances the name *Hezbos* is used in a negative manner or even derogatory manner when speaking about Hezbollah, the noted terror network headquartered in Lebanon. How odd that Dad heard the name *Hezbos*, which indicated to me the Holy Spirit was mocking this group.

Paul taught that we should judge prophetic words (1 Cor. 14:29), and yet Christ taught in Matthew 7:1, "Do not judge, or you too will be judged" (NIV). Is this a contradiction? Paul was instructing believers not just to accept any word as from the Lord, but to weigh it as a group to ensure that the group judging the statement all bore witness to the accuracy of the statement. In Christ's warning not to judge, He was speaking about judging another person's personal life or spirituality, which was a common error among the Pharisees who always were criticizing others for the same sins they themselves were committing and trying to hide.

The closer the body of Christ moves toward the time of the end, the more important the ability to discern will be, for there will not only be false prophets with false words, but also there will arise a higher level of spiritual wickedness that causes a spiritual clash like that between Elijah and the false prophets of Baal!

six

THE PSYCHIC VOICES VERSUS
THE PROPHETIC VISIONS

Give no regard to mediums and familiar spirits;
do not seek after them, to be defiled by them:
I am the LORD your God.

« Leviticus 19:31 »

Whom empires are under spiritual and economic stress and nations flirt with iniquity while playing on the brink of an abyss called *judgment*, there always comes a clash between two kingdoms: the kingdom of God and the kingdom of Satan. It is more than a struggle between political parties called the conservatives and liberals, or divisions caused by two opposite moral views. This clash includes angelic messengers and demonic beings that are assigned in both camps to plot and plan against the opposing side. (See Daniel 10.) We see this battle when two Egyptian magicians, Jannes and Jambres, withstood Moses and duplicated Moses's miracle by turning the rods into serpents (Exod. 7:11–12; 2 Tim. 3:8). Centuries later, Elijah began preaching on Mount Carmel as 850 false prophets failed to pray down fire in the name of the weather god, Baal (1 Kings 18). These "prophets of Baal" were men motivated by compromise who had freely eaten at Queen Jezebel's table and were more concerned with a full belly in a famine than having the fullness of God during the crisis.

Most secular people view spiritual manifestations differently than a believer does. A secularist who hears that a believer was healed by prayer will call the process a *faith healing* and equate the results with some guru living in a hut on foreign soil who claims his followers believed and saw miraculous results. When a secular American with no biblical background hears of a minister of the gospel revealing a detailed word of wisdom or knowledge that comes to pass, the unbeliever will classify the minister as *just another psychic*. Once when I was ministering, a man who was cynical of spiritual manifestations said, "So what is the difference between a psychic telling someone correct information about himself and some preacher telling someone God's future plans?"

I replied, "The difference is that an alleged psychic will tell you what's on your mind, but a man of God will tell you what is on God's mind!"

Years ago a fad was spun that was quite expensive for those people caught in its web. There were alleged psychic phone networks that connected anyone in America with self-acclaimed psychics who were gifted to reveal your most intimate secrets and predict your future. The only stipulation was that it required your credit card to be charged between $3.95 to as high as $4.95 a minute to speak to this *professional* fortune-teller. There were individuals who ran up credit card bills as high as $30,000 after being hooked on their personal psychic. One woman said, "It was amazing. The psychic knew I was going through some emotional problems and that I was struggling with relationships and was having family difficulties." This poor, deceived soul was paying nearly five bucks a minute to have some unknown voice tell her *what she already knew*! It doesn't take a so-called psychic to tell you, "I see some difficulty you are experiencing, and you've had some broken relationships in your past," when about 99.99 percent of the people living have gone through difficulty and broken relationships.

These networks eventually went out of business. One in particular owed more than twenty million dollars for advertising and eventually filed for bankruptcy.[1] I would be quite upset with my *team of psychics* if this was my psychic network. With their ability to predict what was coming, why didn't at least one foresee the future and say, "I see in the future we are going bankrupt…get out of debt!" This is about as ludicrous as a story I heard in the mid-1990s while I was preaching in Modesto, California, about a self-acclaimed psychic who sued a hospital for millions of dollars, alleging that the hospital did an MRI on her brain and she lost her ability to see into the future.[2] If I had been the hospital's attorney, I would have placed the psychic on the stand and asked, "So you can prove you could reveal the future before the MRI?" If she replied yes, then I would ask, "If you were a real revealer of the future, why didn't you know that you would lose your power after you had the MRI?" Case closed!

Most of these networks were actually staffed by men or women operators on the other end who claimed gifts they did not have and who read from scripts while attempting to hold the caller on the line and collect as much money as possible. However, while the majority of these phony psychics could be arrested for false impersonation, there are some individuals who appear to have some form of an ability to *read a person's mind* or to reveal detailed information that is not normally known.

THE RISE OF FAMILIAR SPIRITS

In the early days of nations and empires, and in the infant stage of the nation of Israel, it was common for kings to inquire of men concerning the future. These included astrologers who claimed to read the positioning of the stars, including lunar and solar eclipses, meteorites, and comets. Ancient history could fill volumes with accounts of superstitious leaders who looked to the creation instead of the Creator. Pharaoh had magicians in his court. Nebuchadnezzar was teamed with his astrologers, magicians, and fortune-tellers. These kings believed these fortune-tellers were capable of interpreting dreams, omens, and signs in the sky.

There were, and still are today, times when a psychic, fortune-teller, or a *mind reader* is actually operating with what Scripture calls a "familiar spirit." In the days of Saul, the rebellious king had grieved the Holy Spirit, and God refused to answer Saul's prayer requests. In desperation the king sought out a witch who was operating through the force of a familiar spirit (1 Sam. 28:7, KJV). The witch conducted what is called a *séance*, attempting to bring the spirit of a departed righteous man, Samuel, from the underworld. An aged-looking spirit suddenly appeared to the witch, coming up from below the ground, and Saul *assumed* it was Samuel (1 Sam. 28:7–14). There are disagreements among theologians as to whether this was literally the spirit of Samuel or a familiar spirit imitating Samuel. Most believe the witch saw an apparition of some familiar spirit and the king did not, but the king "perceived that it was Samuel" (v. 14).

The reason for suggesting the spirit was a familiar spirit is because God had refused to answer Saul through known biblical methods such as dreams, prophetic words, or by the Urim (v. 6).

The Law of God forbade contact with witches:

> There shall not be found among you anyone who makes his son or his daughter pass through the fire, or one who practices witchcraft, or a soothsayer, or one who interprets omens, or a sorcerer.
>
> —DEUTERONOMY 18:10

Alleged contact with the dead is called *necromancy*. This was practiced among the heathen nations and empires of antiquity, but it was also forbidden by the Lord in the Law:

> Regard not them that have familiar spirits, neither seek after wizards, to be defiled by them: I am the LORD your God.
>
> —LEVITICUS 19:31, KJV

> There shall not be found among you any one that maketh his son or his daughter to pass through the fire, or that useth divination, or an observer of times, or an enchanter, or a witch. Or a charmer, or a consulter with familiar spirits, or a wizard, or a necromancer.
>
> —DEUTERONOMY 18:10–11, KJV

The English word *necromancer* is supposed to indicate the practice of consulting the dead for the reason of predicting the future. The pagan tribes were very much into worshiping the dead, as was indicated in God's warnings to the Hebrew people. The Almighty told His chosen not to put any "cuttings in your flesh for the dead" (Lev. 19:28, KJV); neither should they make any "baldness between your eyes for the dead" (Deut. 14:1, KJV).

The false notion held among some ancients was that once a person's spirit departed his or her body and entered the next life, that person would be privy to information that was being discussed in the spirit realm, which was not known among those living on the earth. Thus the spirit of the departed was conjured up, and, using the voice of the *medium*, the spirit would speak through the medium and reveal the future. Kings could know if they would win or lose a war (this is the answer Saul was searching for). The biblical truth is that once a person's spirit has departed from the body at death, the spirit of the righteous enters the third heaven in a place called *paradise*, where it waits for the resurrection of the righteous (2 Cor. 12:1–4). If the soul and spirit are from a person who was unrighteous or wicked, when they departed the body, they were carried into a permanent chamber under the earth, where they are separated from God but will be raised to be judged in heaven at the Great White Throne judgment (Rev. 20:11–14). (See my book *Secrets Beyond the Grave* for detailed insight on the subject of life after death.)

How was it possible for a witch or a wizard to divine up information that was accurate and yet not known to the witch or fortune-teller? Some suggest it is a psychic gift. However, the answer is that it is accomplished through a *familiar spirit*. Those in the world of the occult incorrectly believe that a familiar spirit is actually the spirit of a departed loved one who is bringing information from the next world to those friends and family members living. However, this form of alleged spirit contact is forbidden according to the Scripture (Lev. 19:31; 20:6, 27). In Scripture, the Hebrew word for *familiar* is *owb* and is used to describe a hollow sound, such as the sound produced when a person blows into the opening of an old water skin (an animal skin sewed together that held water). It is the same action as when a ventriloquist *throws his voice*, creating the illusion that the puppet on his lap is speaking. This is the same concept for how a person (called a medium) channels a familiar spirit. As the demonic presence enters the room, the medium, sometimes called a *channeler*, opens his or her mouth to speak, and instead of it being that person's normal voice, the pitch changes into a male or female voice. This is because the familiar spirit is "possessing," or taking control of, the physical body in order to communicate the message.

The reason a familiar spirit is called a *familiar* spirit is because it is familiar with the region from which it operates as well as the people and the circumstances that have existed in that region for centuries. We must remember that both angels and demons have existed from the earliest days of mankind. In Revelation we read of Michael the archangel battling Satan and casting the accuser from the second heaven to the earth during the final tribulation (Rev. 12:7–9). Yet we also read where the same angel, Michael, in centuries past, battled Satan for the body of Moses upon the death of the prophet (Jude 9). These two wars were with the same angels, yet more than thirty-five hundred years apart. The angel Gabriel brought heavenly understanding to Daniel, and hundreds of years later appeared to Zacharias and Mary (Dan. 9:21; Luke 1:19–35).

Since both angels and demons are spirit beings, and spirits never age and continually exist from generation to generation, they are familiar with the location, people, and circumstances in the region where they have dwelt and have had rulership for centuries. This may be why when Christ commanded the evil spirits to depart from the possessed man in Mark 5, the spirits requested that Christ would not send them out of the country (the region where they were, Mark 5:10) and that He would not confine them, at that moment, in the "deep," which is "the abyss" or bottomless pit in the Greek (Luke 8:31, KJV). These evil spirits were aware that Christ was the Son of God (Matt. 3:17). This was known from the time of His conception (Luke 1:31–35) to the time of His presentation in the temple (Luke 2:22–38) and during the season of His forty-day temptation prior to His public ministry (Luke 4:1–14). The first prophecy in the Bible was given by God Himself after Adam and Eve sinned in the Garden of Eden. God predicted, "I will put enmity between thee and the woman, and between thy seed and her seed; it shall bruise thy head" (Gen. 3:15, KJV). Thus, the demons knew who Jesus was from the beginning!

When the chief spirit in the possessed man asked Christ not to send them into the "pit" (abyss), how did these spirits know this would be their final place of confinement? After all, it would be more than sixty years later when the apostle John would actually see and record the obituary of Satan and his angels as they were cast into the abyss (the King James Version says "bottomless pit," Rev. 20:1). One Old Testament prophet, Isaiah, predicted that Lucifer would be "brought down... to the lowest depths of the Pit" (Isa. 14:15). We know from the temptation of Christ that Satan is familiar with the Bible, as he quoted a passage in Christ's presence that is found in Psalm 91:10–12. The adversary is also aware that when he is eventually cast out of heaven, he "has a short time" remaining (Rev. 12:12).

This information undergirds my point: the familiar spirits are familiar with information from the past and are able to relate it through the voice of a person who opens himself or herself up to being controlled or possessed by these spirits. In what is called the New Age movement, individuals connect to spirits by *channeling* them in their bodies. Some claim these are *ascended masters* from the past whose spirits roam through the cosmos and bring super-natural or divine insight into the cosmic mysteries linked with life. I have read occasional stories of some who claim that ancient Indians have given them insights from the past, and the information revealed later proved accurate through detailed historical research. This alleg-edly *proves* that these spirits are the spirits of ancient men and women. In reality, it *proves* no such thing when you understand the operation of a familiar spirit.

However, these incidents do prove that the spirit world is real. These manifestations are not the spirits of the departed; they are demonic entities that have existed since the fall of Satan. Any *past information* can be revealed to a medium who channels the evil spirit. The deception comes, for example, when a family member who lost a loved one through death consults a medium who claims to be able to make contact with the departed soul of that person's loved one. Once the process begins, the spirit begins to speak about an event in the person's life or accurately names several family mem-bers. The family member is overwhelmed with joy to know that he or she can contact the loved one. At times the family member will even be told certain things to do to make this *spirit* happy or at peace.

For several years a famed psychic hosted a popular television program during which he claimed to make contact with the dead. Sometimes I would watch how he manipulated a question to get a certain response or would *hit and miss* until he could finally put together a story line that the family agreed was a message from the next world.

In the Bible we do read where Moses (who had died) and Elijah (who was translated) appeared to Christ (Matt. 17:1–4). This was a rare instance and was under the supervision of God Himself. Christ did not conjure up these men, but God sent them to reveal informa-tion to Christ. However, the law of God in Scripture totally forbids the use of mediums, soothsayers, fortune-tellers, and witchcraft in any and all forms.

Witchcraft is nothing to play with and is a very dangerous spiritual bridge over dark waters that a believer should never cross. A believer must rely upon biblical methods to receive spiritual insight, direction, and the path for the future.

We can all be assured that Christ will return (1 Thess. 4:16–17). The righteous dead will be raised at the resurrection (1 Cor. 15:52). Heaven does exist, and we will see the New Jerusalem (Rev. 22). And we will rule and reign with Christ for a thousand years if we are faithful (Rev. 20:1–4).

In those areas where a personal prayer requires an answer, we must rely upon the promises of God's Word and understand that He can reveal Himself to us—primarily through the Scriptures and, at various times and seasons, through His Holy Spirit's gifts (1 Cor. 12:7–10) or through a dream or a vision.

THE *REAL* PROPHETIC

Turning our attention from the false to the real, it is important for believers to understand that God can and will reveal truth to His children. Paul wrote in 1 Corinthians 14 that believers can speak by "revelation" (vv. 6, 26). This word in Greek is *apokalupsis* and alludes to something hidden that is disclosed and made known. Prior to Christ's suffering, resurrection, and ascension, He encouraged His disciples by predicting that when He departed from them, He would send "another Comforter," which is the Holy Spirit (John 14:16, KJV; 16:7, KJV). The Holy Spirit would "teach them all things, and bring to your remembrance all things that I said to you" (John 14:26), and He would "tell you things to come" (John 16:13). It is very contradictory that although many mainline churches believe the Holy Spirit is the Comforter and the Teacher who assists in your ability to recall the

Scriptures, using passages from John's Gospel to prove their point, yet the part about "telling you things to come" is omitted at times. It is only used to exclaim that He reveals the correct interpretation of Bible prophecy to you. All of this is correct, but the Holy Spirit also provides believers with warnings and instruction through the inward leading of the Spirit and as we pray with understanding or in the Spirit (Rom. 8:26–28; 1 Cor. 14:14–15).

The Book of Acts is called *the Acts of the Apostles*. However, it is actually the Acts of the Holy Spirit! Without the power of the Holy Spirit, there would be few acts of the apostles! The nine gifts mentioned in 1 Corinthians 12 are not the *gifts of the apostles* but the "gifts of the Holy Spirit," and they will continue until the return of the Lord (1 Cor. 1:7). The Almighty began His story with man by walking with Adam in the Garden of Eden, and there was never a time in the four thousand years from Adam to Christ that God was not revealing Himself or His truth to a people. The Bible is the final written revelation from God, and there are no *new truths* beyond the revelation of Scripture; but there is fresh insight from old truth. Christ taught:

> Then He said to them, "Therefore every scribe instructed concerning the kingdom of heaven is like a householder who brings out of his treasure things new and old."
>
> —MATTHEW 13:52

The revelation the Holy Spirit brings forth involves situations occurring now or in the future. At times you enter a season where you are uncertain of the will of God or of how to handle a difficult circumstance. Wisdom can be given by a revelation through the gift of the word of wisdom or the word of knowledge (1 Cor. 12:8). When a believer needs a word of encouragement or comfort, a prophetic word for "edification and exhortation and comfort" can be received—sometimes through preaching, or through a song, or through an individual (1 Cor. 14:3).

Believers should never seek the counterfeit methods of men working through familiar spirits but must look to the Word of God and the operation of the Holy Spirit for insight into God's will and purpose. Throughout the New Testament, warnings were given in advance to prepare believers for what was coming. A prophet named Agabus warned the church that a severe drought was coming and the saints should prepare to send relief to those in need (Acts 11:28–29). The same man revealed by the Holy Spirit that if Paul went to the temple in Jerusalem, he would be arrested and delivered into the hands of the Gentiles (Acts 21:10–12). On another occasion Paul was being sent by ship to Rome. He was warned in his spirit that if the ship loosed from the dock, there would be severe consequences (Acts 27:9–10). Later the ship hit a storm, and the lives of the entire crew were in danger. After fourteen days of no sun or stars, Paul received a vision of an angel that predicted the ship would be torn apart, but the entire crew of 276 men would survive the shipwreck (vv. 22–44).

The entire Bible is a book of revelation. The Hebrew nation was formed as a result of angelic visitations, dreams, and visions.

AMAZING ANCIENT DREAMS

Joseph, the son of Jacob, was sold by his brothers to the Ishmaelites and then later sold to an Egyptian to be his personal slave. By interpreting two warning dreams, Joseph was exalted by Pharaoh as second in command over the land of Egypt. Joseph eventually married the daughter of an Egyptian priest named Asenath (Gen. 41:45). Scripture says that Joseph had a silver cup used to "practice divination" or to reveal the future (Gen. 44:2, 15). Pharaoh most likely gave this cup to Joseph for Joseph's interpretation of his dream. There is no record that it was ever used or needed, since Joseph was directed by the Spirit of God.

A believer should never consult a secular source for words of instruction, as God only works through His Word and the Holy Spirit. Even the ancient wise men, soothsayers, and astrologers of biblical history were helpless to interpret the dreams and visions given to Pharaoh, Nebuchadnezzar, and other men (Gen. 41:8; Dan. 2:10). Only the Holy Spirit can interpret the revelations given from the heavenly Father (John 16:13). When Nebuchadnezzar had the troubling dream of the metallic image and could not recall what he had dreamed, his own wise men said, "There is no other who can tell it to the king except the gods, whose dwelling is not with flesh" (Dan. 2:11). Thus, it took Daniel, a man full of the Holy Spirit and wisdom, to interpret the dream. The same is true today!

In the days of Sesostris II (1906–1887 B.C.), the priest of Heilopolis had a vision he recorded. The words appear to be a prediction:

> He sees the ideal ruler for whose advent he longs.... "He brings cooling to the flame. It is said he is the shepherd of all men. There is no evil in his heart....Where is he to-day?...Behold his might is not seen."[3]

The Hebrews were shepherds, and Egyptians hated shepherds (Gen. 46:34). When Joseph requested that his estranged brothers meet Pharaoh, he instructed them that when the king asked about their occupations, they reply, "We raise cattle." The brothers instead chose to reveal they were shepherds. Joseph may have been fearful that Pharaoh would restrict his family from living in Egypt, since the predicted future leader was called a "shepherd."

There was also an ancient prediction from a dream concerning a lamb that would defeat Egypt. This account comes from Adam Clarke's commentary:

Jonathan ben Uzziel gives us a curious reason for the command given by Pharaoh to the Egyptian women: "Pharaoh slept, and saw in his sleep a balance, and behold the whole land of Egypt stood in one scale, and a lamb in the other; and the scale in which the lamb was outweighed that in which was the land of Egypt. Immediately he sent and called all the chief magicians, and told them his dream. And Janes [*sic*] and Jambres, (see 2 Tim. 3:8) who were chief of the magicians, opened their mouths and said to Pharaoh, 'A child is shortly to be born in the congregation of the Israelites, whose hand shall destroy the whole land of Egypt.' Therefore Pharaoh spake to the midwives, etc."[4]

The Jewish historian Josephus wrote this:

One of those sacred scribes [said to be Jannes or Jambres in the Targum of Jonathan], who are very sagacious in foretelling future events truly, told the king, that about this time there would a child be born to the Israelites, who, if he were reared, would bring Egyptian dominion low, and would raise the Israelites; that he would excel all men in virtue, and obtain a glory that would be remembered though all ages. Which thing was so feared by the king, that, according to this man's opinion, he commanded that they should cast every male child, which was born to the Israelites, into the river, and destroy it...that if any parents should disobey him and venture to save their male children alive, they and their families should be destroyed.[5]

It would truly be a lamb that would defeat the entire empire of Egypt. This lamb was the Passover lamb offered at each house prior to the Exodus (Exod. 12). The lamb's blood was placed in the left, right, and top outer parts of the door to prevent the destroyer from taking the life of the firstborn sons (v. 7). The lamb was then roasted and eaten, bringing healing to the entire Hebrew nation all in one night (Ps. 105:37). That night all of the Egyptians' firstborn among the people, the animals, and the captives died (Exod. 12:29).

A VISION BEFORE MOSES'S BIRTH

The Jewish historian Josephus records that Moses's father, Amram, had a lengthy dream (vision) in which God appeared to him and exhorted him not to despair concerning the future. In the vision, God previewed Hebrew history from Abraham, Isaac, and Jacob and informed Amram that He was with these men in all their ways. He predicted that Amram's child (Moses) would deliver the Hebrew nation and would be concealed from danger. His memory would be famous while the world would last. The vision revealed that this child would also have a brother who would obtain a God-ordained priesthood, and his posterity would have it after him to the end of the world.[6] Thus, the birth of one of the world's greatest deliverers was preceded by a prophetic dream.

Three years before the birth of Moses, there was a conjunction of Jupiter and Saturn, which occurred in the constellation Pisces (the fish). Pisces has always been considered to be a sign of the nation of the Hebrews (Israel). This was interpreted as a sign that a great person was born among the Jews. Some rabbis suggest this was the motive for Pharaoh instructing the midwives to kill male children by throwing them into the Nile River (Exod. 1:22). The alligator was one of the gods of Egypt, and slaying the Hebrew infants could serve as an offering to another Egyptian god. God had the final word. About eighty years later, the Egyptian army was drowned in the Red Sea (Exod. 14).

Julius Caesar was the first emperor of imperial Rome. He passed laws that caused people to move from one location to another. One such group was colonists from Capua. While constructing buildings they came across ancient graves and found vessels and began searching them. In the tomb of Capys, the founder of Capua, was a brass tablet with a prediction recorded in Greek which read:

> Whenever the bones of Capys come to be discovered, a descendant of Iulus will be slain by the hands of his kinsmen, and his death revenged by fearful disasters throughout Italy.[7]

Julius Caesar's wife, Calpurnia, had a troubling *dream* that their home fell apart and warned her husband not to go to the Senate. He ignored the warning and was stabbed twenty-three times, dying at age fifty-six in 44 B.C.[8] Thus the strange prediction, made years before, came to pass. The fellow should have heeded his wife's warning.

Never doubt God's ability to speak today and to bring the insight needed for your protection, direction, and inspiration, and never follow counterfeit men and methods that offer deception.

seven

CAN A WARNING DREAM BE ALTERED THROUGH PRAYER?

So I sought for a man among them who would make a wall, and stand in the gap before Me on behalf of the land, that I should not destroy it; but I found no one.

« Ezekiel 22:30 »

T here have been countless believers who have experienced a dream with a warning of coming danger, a threat to their life, or a satanic attack that was being plotted against them. One of the most common and most important questions asked is: "When you receive a warning of coming danger through a dream (or a vision), is it possible to alter the situation and prevent it from occurring?"

Let's begin by considering prophetic warnings in the Scripture. When Moses was given the Torah (the Bible's first five books), the prophet told the people of Israel that if they disobeyed the commandments and laws of God, they would be given the opportunity to repent and prevent judgment from overtaking them. However, he warned them that if they persisted in their sins and continued their rejection of God's divine instructions, they would be taken captive by their enemies, drought would destroy their crops, their animals would suffer, and they would see the consequences of their disobedience. (See Deuteronomy 28; Leviticus 26.)

In Israel's history, God did not immediately move His hand from mercy to judgment. There was always a gap of time that gave the people opportunity to turn or repent. Christ warned the church at Thyatira that a self-acclaimed female "prophetess" was seducing God's servants. She and the entire church were given "time to repent," and if they refused, a "great tribulation" would come upon them (Rev. 2:21–22). Year after year, generation after generation, Israel continued its rejection of God's commandments, and so the Almighty predicted that the nation would be taken into captivity in Babylon for seventy years (Jer. 25:11). Once the time frame for this judgment had been set, it eventually came to pass.

When Christ predicted that the temple (Matt. 24:1–2) and Jerusalem would be destroyed within one generation (Matt 23:34–36), He also revealed that He would have often gathered the city and the people together as a hen gathers her chicks under her wings, but the people refused (v. 37). Once the sands in the hourglass of grace reached their end, the glass was shattered along with the sand. It was while the nation was still under great prosperity that Isaiah and Jeremiah both predicted the Babylonian captivity. Eventually the prosperity ceased, and Jerusalem was left in smoldering ruins. Some false prophets were predicting that God loved Jerusalem too much to allow its demise. The deceitful dreams of these false dreamers also went up in smoke.

Warnings and mercy always precede judgment. In Scripture, the warnings came through angelic visitations (Gen. 19), dreams, and visions, or they were pronounced by a prophet. Many of the warnings we receive in a dream (or vision) are not geared to an international, national, or city judgment, but they are usually warnings for individuals, their families, or their churches. Many warning dreams deal with future spiritual, emotional, physical, or economic difficulties. In these cases intense prayer can possibly prevent the attack or alter the circumstances.

I SAW HIM—THEN HE DIED

There is also a danger of accepting what you see with a rather "whatever will be will be" attitude and not standing in the gap through prayer. Shortly after my wife and I were married, I was ministering for Pastor Tony Scott in Sylvania, Ohio (Toledo area). Pam and I were staying at Pastor Scott's home. During those early days, I would stay up until two or three in the morning, studying and at times praying. On this night I went to bed around 2:00 a.m., and shortly after lying down and attempting to sleep, I saw a very brief, full-color scene of a man standing before me. He wore a plaid shirt, old blue jeans, and brown leather boots. He was clearly staring at me. I was so stunned that I sat up and said to my wife, "I just saw a man who attends your home church!" When I described him to her, she knew whom I was talking about, but neither of us could recall his name. I spent about fifteen minutes trying to remember his name. Finally I lay down, and for the *second time* I saw an exact repeat of the same image. There he was, looking at me wearing the same clothes.

Again, I woke up and said, "I just saw him again! What is all this about?" I did not see anything or anyone else. I never prayed for him or asked the Lord why I saw him so clearly in this vision (it was not a dream).

The following afternoon, my wife spoke to her sister in Northport, Alabama, my wife's hometown. Her sister Shelia said, "Pam, did anyone call you and tell you about Bill Ward?"

"No," Pam responded, "who is that?" When Shelia described him, Pam replied, "Oh my, that's his name. That's the man the Lord touched in Perry's four-week revival at the church!"

Shelia proceeded to tell us that early that morning (a few hours after I saw him), Bill was returning from work when he lost control of his truck, was thrown out, and was killed! We were both in shock. It was months later when I spoke with his widow and described the clothes he wore in the vision—which she confirmed he was wearing the morning of his death.

At the time I did not know the spiritual law of the "double dream," or how in a double dream the event is established and will came to pass. Time and experience are valuable twins that teach us truth and how to discern events and how to pray. When Israel sinned with the golden calf, it was the intent of God to destroy the entire nation of Israel and leave one man alive—Moses (Exod. 32:8–10), thus raising up a nation through this faithful prophet. Moses immediately reminded the Lord of His covenant with Abraham, Isaac, and Jacob, and how the heathen nations would mock God's name and accuse Him of bringing Israel out of Egypt to slay them in the desert (vv. 11–13). After being reminded of His promise to Abraham to bring his children out of Egypt and back to the Promised Land, the Bible says, "The LORD repented of the evil which he thought to do unto his people" (Exod. 32:14, KJV). God was not *repenting of sin* but was simply changing His mind concerning His plans. The prayer of Moses changed the direction of God!

When the Almighty informed Abraham that He was planning on destroying the cities of the plain, including Sodom and Gomorrah, God's covenant man Abraham began a deep discussion with the Lord to negotiate for the safety of the righteous who may be living among the unrighteous in the city. Abraham began with fifty people, and God promised to preserve the wicked city if He could find just fifty in the city. Soon the number dropped to ten, and God agreed to stop the destruction if ten righteous people were found in Sodom (Gen. 18:23–33). This action taken by Abraham is called *intercession*. The act of interceding is when one person stands in place for another to prevent the other person from experiencing judgment, danger, or destruction. For example, Christ is now in the heavenly temple, standing to represent us as our eternal High Priest, and He "always lives to make intercession for them" (Heb. 7:25). An intercessor is one who makes a petition on behalf of another. In our case, when we sin we need a person who serves as a *lawyer* (called an *advocate* in 1 John 2:1) to represent us in heaven, because Satan, the "accuser of the brethren," much like a prosecutor in a courtroom, is continually hurling accusations before the eternal throne against us (Rev. 12:10).

We have an intercessor in heaven, Jesus Christ, and a Comforter on the earth, the Holy Spirit (John 14:16, 26). My precious father had taught me for years that a warning dream does not always mean that what you see is set to happen and cannot be prevented. But the dream can be given so that the person receiving it can *pray to prevent the event from coming to pass.*

LEARNING TO LISTEN TO YOUR WIFE'S WARNING DREAMS

While he was sitting on the judgment seat, his wife
sent to him, saying, "Have nothing to do with that
just Man, for I have suffered many things today in
a dream because of Him."

« Matthew 27:19 »

One of the most interesting, yet often overlooked, warning dreams in the Bible involved a wife who gave a warning to her husband about his treatment of Jesus. During the public trial of Christ, a raging mob of religious zealots was demanding Christ's execution. The biblical narrative begins with Pilate, a man appointed by Rome to be the governor in the region of Judea. Before any death penalty could be enacted, Pilate would need to condemn Christ. Just as Pilate was preparing to judge Christ and condemn Him to be put to death, Pilate's wife sent a message saying that she had a troubling dream of Christ that showed Him to be an innocent man.

No detail is given in the Scripture as to what she dreamed or why she "suffered many things." The *suffering* was not a physical pain but was a mental or an emotional stress that she experienced as a result of her dream. In Scripture she is simply called "Pilate's wife," but church tradition says that she was a believer in Christ and was later named as Saint Procula, or, as some suggest, Saint Claudia. The early father Origen, in his *Homilies on Matthew*, suggests that she became a Christian. There is a suggestion that in Paul's last letter to Timothy (2 Tim. 4:21), the Claudia he alludes to may refer to Pilate's wife, who became a believer. The Eastern Orthodox and Ethiopian Orthodox churches celebrate her in the church each year. Hundreds of years later, a letter written in Latin says that she actually sought out Christ to heal her son Pilo's crippled foot.[1]

Did Pilate pay attention to his wife's warning? Apparently something moved him not to condemn Jesus. In fact, Pilate publicly said that Christ was "just" (Matt. 27:24). When the raging crowd demanded that Christ be crucified, Pilate offered to release a prisoner to them. I suggest that Pilate was hoping they would release Jesus. However, they demanded instead that Barabbas, a thief, be released (vv. 16–21). Christ was later crucified between two thieves. Barabbas, who was scheduled for execution with his two cohorts, was to hang on the third cross on Mount Calvary, but instead, the middle cross was prepared for Christ!

Pilate then asked for a basin of water and washed his hands—attempting to free himself of the guilt of innocent blood (v. 24). This was a procedure known to the religious Jews, based upon instruction in Deuteronomy, requiring that when a corpse is discovered near a city, the elders living closest to that city are to take a heifer, cut off its head, and wash their hands in water over the slain heifer while declaring that they are innocent of the blood of the slain corpse (Deut. 21:3–6). Pilate did not ask for a heifer, but he did wash his hands, and the Jewish religious authorities knew what he was doing. He was declaring himself free from the blood of Christ, which was about to be shed. It was at that moment that the religious Jews said, "His blood be on us and on our children" (Matt. 27:25). According to the Law of Moses, this brought a curse upon the city of Jerusalem and the land of Israel, as Christ indicated was possible when there was a continual shedding of the blood of innocents and the righteous (Matt. 23:34–36).

Clearly, something emboldened Pilate not to agree with the death sentence that the multitude was screaming out should be placed upon Christ. I believe he was moved by his wife's warning dream.

THE INSTINCT OF A WOMAN

Married couples often make jokes about the fact that a wife has a certain type of *inner instinct* that seems to be missing in the average husband. This *inner radar* (as some call it) is unique when considering that Eve was seduced by the serpent in the garden (2 Cor. 11:3). The adversary's crafty, smooth words inspired the woman to eat from a forbidden tree (Gen. 3:1–7). This may be the one weakness in the female nature. Normally a woman is not moved so much by the physical appearance of a man as she is by the care, compassion, affection, and *kind words* he expresses. I have often said that if the serpent had been a female, Eve would have chased the snake from the garden while beating it on the head with a stick and screaming, "Get out of here, you lying woman—you're just trying to steal my man!"

Men (husbands) can be very rational in their thinking process and often lack the discernment that a wife can sense in her spirit. I have a side hobby, of which the inspiration for it often comes and goes. I enjoy writing songs and have been blessed to have had more than forty songs published and sung on numerous CDs. Many years ago my wife and I were friends with a young married couple who were traveling ministers. The man was a dynamic preacher, and his wife accompanied him, often singing in the meetings. She asked me if I would like to work with her on her new musical CD project, using some of my songs. Of course I was thrilled with the prospect of getting my songs out, and even creating more music that would bless many people.

I approached my wife, and she said it was fine, that we could work at the ministry office on the project.

However, late that night my wife had a very troubling dream. It was actually a twofold warning. In the first dream, she saw this very woman in a very compromising situation and saw me in the distance. Pam felt this woman was, as we used to say, "scoping me out" in a seductive manner. She then dreamed of a large tarantula that was approaching an area where Pam was standing near a high fence. Pam took a small dagger and drove it into the heart of this large spider. The next morning she related the dream to me, and we researched this type of spider to see if there was some *spiritual understanding* as to why she saw a tarantula. We discovered that this kind of spider slowly weaves its web to capture its prey and leads its prey into a slow death.

Pam felt this was linked to the woman, and she said, "I don't feel good about the idea of her working around you. I think she is going to try to weave a slow web and pull you in." Because my wife seldom dreams, and when she does it usually contains a meaning, I immediately told the woman that it would not work out to assist her, but I could recommend some individuals who could help with her project. Both Pam and I felt we made a wise decision.

A few months later it was discovered that this woman was actually having numerous affairs. Imagine the shock when we received a phone call from a close pastor friend who shared with us a terrible encounter that had occurred between this woman and a male member of his church while this woman's husband was ministering in their church. God spared me from perhaps a moral disaster or, at the least, a possible emotional attack with this dream.

PAY ATTENTION, FELLOWS

The female radar is very effective in pinpointing the hidden motives of other women. My wife has often said, "No one knows a woman like another woman." As a man, this female instinct amazes me, especially in understanding how this *gift* is possible and how it works. However, in every instance when my wife (who is a very spiritual and praying woman) has given me a warning, it was later proven to be accurate. Ministers will often mention numerous women in the Bible who were masters of seduction, such as Delilah, who gave Samson the world's most destructive haircut, or Jezebel, who was a seducer of men in the early church (Judges 16; Rev. 2:20). However, women like Anna, Mary, and her cousin Elizabeth were all sensitive to the leading of the Holy Spirit. Anna was the first female prophetess to see the infant Christ, as Simeon the rabbi announced that

Jesus was the anticipated Jewish Messiah (Luke 2:36–38). Mary was receptive to the angel who announced that she, as a virgin, would conceive a child (Luke 1:30–35), and Elizabeth, the aged, barren wife of a priest, became pregnant through a supernatural visitation (vv. 1–25). These were all women of great faith whose names are memorialized in the Bible and in the history of the Christian church.

MY MOTHER'S DREAM

My mother, Juanita Stone, was blessed with three children—Diana, myself, and Phillip—and at age thirty-nine she became pregnant with her fourth child. Because she had a C-section when delivering each of her previous three children, when her doctor discovered she was six weeks pregnant, he immediately suggested three options to her: she should have a test to help determine the health of the child, or she should abort the *fetus* because there was a high risk that the child may have severe physical or mental birth defects, plus the great danger there was to her with the pregnancy, or, a third choice, she could take a chance and continue the pregnancy. My mother informed the doctor that aborting the child—although she was *only six weeks pregnant*, was not an option. The doctor said she would need to make a decision before the third month of pregnancy.

Mother meant it when she said, "Abortion is not an option." She also knew that there were numerous physical and medical indicators that leaned toward this being a high-risk pregnancy with a high possibility that the child would be born mentally challenged. Mom began to pray, knowing that God foreknew she would become pregnant and that He knew she would be forty when the child was born. Yet He permitted the conception to occur. During her time of seeking the Lord, it was a *dream* that confirmed her confession of faith.

She dreamed that she saw a child, a beautiful girl with curly hair. She knew this was the child in her womb. In the dream the child was not sick, feeble, or deformed but was in perfect health. When Mom returned to the doctor, she told him the Lord showed her she would have a healthy baby girl with curly hair. Of course you can imagine his skepticism. He viewed her as an overly zealous Christian woman who was denying the medical facts that were now facing her.

The pregnancy—near death

Mom carried the child full term. When the time came for delivery, it was discovered she had a severe blockage in her intestines, and the doctors wanted to perform emergency surgery. But mother's strength was gone. She began to bleed profusely in the delivery room, and it came to a point where the doctor felt he was *losing her*. Mom actually experienced an *out-of-body experience* in which her soul (or spirit) came out of her body. She was hovering above, looking down upon the doctor and nurses working on her to stop the bleeding. This occurred on a Sunday. I was a teenager at the time. A call came to Dad's church (he was a pastor) to pray for Mom. I didn't know at the time that I almost lost my mother. However, Mother lived and gave birth to that little curly-headed girl, Melanie Dawn Stone. My mother, now in her seventies, still works part-time at my office, and my *little* sister, now in her thirties, is one of our data-entry personnel. God used this dream to remove fear and confirm Mom's faith. When things became difficult, she would remind the Lord of the promise He gave her.

ANOTHER PREGNANCY DREAM

One of the most dramatic demonstrations of the power of a woman's dream that my wife and I still occasionally discuss occurred many years ago and involved a very dear and well-known minister and his wife. I had been on an overseas trip and was returning to Atlanta Hartsfield Airport, where my wife was waiting at the baggage claim. When we were driving out of the airport, she said, "I had a dream. I believe the Lord wants us to go visit this couple in their service tonight." In the dream, Pam saw this pastor's wife crying as she sat in a restroom. She was troubled because she had learned she was pregnant. She was saying, "I can't go through with this." Pam saw that the woman was very distressed, and a heavy depression had overwhelmed her. Pam commented, "I think she's pregnant, and I must go and tell her this dream and tell her it will be all right." Without the couple's knowledge that we were coming, we drove for quite some time and arrived just after the Wednesday night service had begun. The pastor saw us in the audience and welcomed us to the service. His wife was not in her normal seat. Pam said, "I don't think she is here, but her mother is. I'll speak with her after service."

After service Pam spoke to the woman's mother, who said, "Pam, guess what…she is pregnant again!" Pam turned pale and replied, "I must tell you this dream," which she proceeded to do. The mother began weeping, saying, "You must go see her. She is so depressed, she didn't come to church tonight. The Lord sent you to her!" After telling the pastor the dream, he began to cry and said, "You both have no idea what we have been through the past several weeks. I have almost quit pastoring because of the stress I've been under."

That night we arrived at their house to the surprise of the wife! We sat down with her and her husband, and Pam related in detail the dream and began to share from her heart. What Pam saw had literally occurred the night she dreamed it! My wife is a very quiet and a behind-the-scenes person, yet I was so proud of her for obeying the Lord. Not only did the Holy Spirit touch the couple that night, but also the pregnancy went great. That infant is now a beautiful young woman who is wholly dedicated to the Lord!

What if Pam had *ignored the dream* and said, "I had a really stupid dream the other night," or was not sensitive to discern the warning of the Holy Spirit? It is possible that the stress upon the couple could have moved them out of the perfect will of God.

Women tend to be more spiritually minded and sensitive than most men. This is witnessed in the two visitations of the angel Gabriel: one to a male priest named Zacharias, and the other to the Virgin Mary. When Gabriel stood at the temple's golden altar announcing that Zacharias's barren wife would conceive a son, Zacharias required a *sign* that the event would happen! His sign for his unbelief was that he was unable to speak during his wife's pregnancy—for nine months (Luke 1:1-20). Mary was also informed that she would become pregnant with a son, and her attitude was, "Let it be to me according to your word" (Luke 1:38). The *preacher* was skeptical of an angelic messenger, and the simple handmaiden from Nazareth was ready to believe what seemed impossible! When Christ was crucified, the disciples ran for their lives (with the exception of John); however, the women stuck with Him until the end (Mark 15:40-41). At the tomb, it was three women who were plotting to remove a massive stone to anoint the body (Mark 16:1-4), since no men were among them, as the disciples were hiding behind closed doors in fear. Some of the chief financial supporters of Christ's ministry were women:

> …and certain women who had been healed of evil spirits and infirmities—Mary called Magdalene, out of whom had come seven demons, and Joanna the wife of Chuza, Herod's steward, and Susanna, and many others who provided for Him from their substance.
>
> —Luke 8:2-3

Men tend to think in the realm of logic, and in Western culture, men are often taught from the time they are boys not to express their emotions, especially in the form of crying or being overly humble. This tends to make men uncomfortable with religious expression, especially if it involves holding another guy's hand in a church service when *agreeing in prayer* or expressing their emotions through tears. Women, on the other hand, are created with the ability to show more empathy, compassion, and intuition because they are more closely in touch with their emotions. Most have no difficulty flowing with soothing words, hugs, kisses, tenderness, and crying when the occasion deems necessary. Religion may come across as formal and dry in its approach, but an experience with God brings an encounter with righteousness, peace, and joy in the Holy Spirit (Rom. 14:17). If a husband is married to a dedicated, praying, believing woman, then he should learn to pay attention to her inner senses, her nudges, and those dreams from time to time, as well as those feelings she may seem to bug you about.

If a husband was to ask himself, "Why doesn't the Lord show me what He is showing my wife?" the answer might be, "Your spiritual antenna is not up the way hers is."

DON'T ABUSE THE GIFT

It is very important that every Christian woman understands and guards this unique ability and never abuses it, especially in the area of attempting to *control* your companion. You must never allow fleshly jealousy to be interpreted as some *feeling* you have toward someone, when in reality you are jealous of the other person's favor or blessings. In the Book of Judges, a woman named Delilah was paid to gain secret information from a man named Samson. Knowing that a seductive woman could make a fellow do things that they would normally never do, Delilah continually pressed Samson with her words: "Tell me your secret...tell me where your strength comes from...tell me or you don't love me...you really don't love me if you don't give me what I want." (See Judges 16.) Samson had killed a lion and destroyed a thousand Philistines, but he couldn't handle the continual verbal wearing down he received from his forbidden Philistine girlfriend who owned the local beauty salon in Gaza.

One of the great dangers that have existed for centuries in the Christian church is the abuse of spiritual gifts. Church history is replete with individuals who claimed to be prophets and led people astray with some alleged prophetic inspiration or warning. In my book *Unusual Prophecies Being Fulfilled*, book number 7, I wrote:

> It was in the late sixteenth century. Along the rivers and lakes in Austria and Germany, they were building arks. They were mostly simply farmers using hammer, nails, and hewn trees, building large boats to protect their families from another "global flood," similar to the flood of Noah's day. The people were following the prophetic instructions of an astrologer and self-acclaimed prophet, Johann Stoffler. According to the irrefutable calculations of Stoffler, another massive flood was about to strike all of Europe, and the only survivors of this deadly deluge were those following his instruction to prepare arks for the saving of their families.
>
> The date arrived and went without any storms, floods, or destruction. In retrospect, if the commoners had possessed Bibles and could have read God's promise to Noah every time they saw a rainbow draping the sky, they would have known that God made a covenant never to destroy the earth by water again (Gen. 9:13–16). People began looking for answers, and another astronomer entered the scene, another alleged prophet from Vienna, Austria, named Georg Tannenstetter, and disproved the

calculation of Stoffler and declared no flood would come. Oh well, so much for the houseboats.[2]

If an individual has been gifted to hear from the Lord, then he or she must guard against using this gift in the wrong manner or even participating in merchandising of the gift for personal gain, which is forbidden in Scripture:

> And many will follow their destructive ways, because of whom the way of truth will be blasphemed. By covetousness they will exploit you with deceptive words; for a long time their judgment has not been idle, and their destruction does not slumber.
>
> —2 PETER 2:2–3

There are so-called *prophets* who ask for payment (*offerings*) in exchange for a word from the Lord. I heard of one person who allegedly interprets dreams, charging the person for the interpretation. Legitimate ministries and churches that operate on tithes and offerings according to this *charging* are simply merchandising God, and this is displeasing to God!

One reason to express this warning is because there have been women in the past who became so *spiritual* in their own eyes that they left their children and husbands for their own *ministry*. They began believing that their families were interfering with the *gift* God had given them for the world. May I suggest this, ladies: do not be getting on a bus that is heading to Washington DC to *bind the evil spirits over our nation* when you cannot deal with the little spirits affecting your home or your own personal life. Women, if you are married with children, then your first priority is to be a mother to your children and a wife to your husband. I want to strongly say that God does not need *your gift* badly enough for you to leave your children without a mother and hit the road for the kingdom. (See 1 Corinthians 7.)

Whatever form of gift God has imparted to you, follow the Lord with all meekness and humility, seeking to be a blessing to others, and always give God glory for all He performs through you.

nine

WHAT IT MEANS WHEN DREAMING OF A DEPARTED LOVED ONE

We are confident, yes, well pleased rather to be absent from the body and to be present with the Lord.

« 2 Corinthians 5:8 »

The death of a close friend or a loved one is a sorrowful and often traumatic experience. The emptiness that prevails and the loneliness that is felt, caused by their absence, can be emotionally overwhelming. Many people long to hear that familiar voice, that warm laughter, or the departed speak to them again. At times the grieving person will receive comfort from a dream in which the departed person appears to be speaking with them. There have been many questions sent to me about what it means when an individual sees a departed loved one in a dream.

My grandfather John Bava was a minister, songwriter, book publisher, and multigifted man whom I admired greatly. He went to be with Christ in 1998. Since that time, seldom a week goes by that I don't have a dream that he is in. At times we are at the old home place in West Virginia. Other times I see him with Grandmother, and we are on a farm, sitting with the family eating or just hearing him laugh. After a loved one, especially a believer, passes away, it is quite common for a close family member to dream about that person. Part of this is because the individual is locked forever in your memory vault and a permanent image is imprinted in your heart. Anyone who has been an active part of your life remains in the seat of your spirit, whether they are living or deceased. In fact, there are times when it seems as though my grandfather and grandmother are still with us, although we know their spirits are in the presence of the Lord (2 Cor. 5:8).

Out of the many times I have seen Granddad, they were simply a dream. There was no particular meaning to the dream, and I was rather joyful when I awoke to remember him as a part of my life. Oddly, however, there have been occasions when the Lord would allow a person who has departed to appear in a dream to a loved one, at times to bring comfort. One of the most dramatic incidents that I know occurred years ago in Tuscumbia, Alabama. I was ministering in a local church, and an elderly woman told me of this personal incident. She and her husband had been believers for many years. He suddenly and unexpectedly passed away. She came to a point where she needed some additional income to pay bills. When living, her husband told her he had hidden some money in the house in the event of an emergency, but the fellow never told her where the money was hidden. She had looked in drawers, in the cupboard, and other areas and found nothing. She cried out to the Lord to help her and to reveal—if there was money in the house—where it was hidden. One night she awoke and saw her husband standing near the foot of her bed. She was stunned! He said nothing but walked toward the bedroom closet and pointed to a stack of blankets. He turned and pointed to the bottom blanket several times, smiled, and then vanished. She came to herself and didn't know if she had dreamed this or if it was a vision.

To *test this spirit* to see if it was from the Lord (1 John 4:1), she arose and went to the closet. She pulled down a stack of blankets on the top shelf. As she laid them on the bed and began opening them, she opened the bottom blanket, and there were thousands of dollars folded in the blanket! Obviously the Lord was concerned for this precious widow, and He knew where the money was. The Lord used a dream-vision to bring her what she requested. Notice that she did not ask to see her husband, but she asked for God to reveal the location of the money. However, God used this event to encourage and bless her.

DAD'S SUPERNATURAL CALL INTO THE MINISTRY

The most dramatic encounter I know of as it relates to the Lord allowing someone to see the spirit of a departed loved one was my own father. For many years Dad has retold the story over and over of the day when he was called into the ministry as a teenager.

Dad was converted at age seventeen and began hosting prayer meetings with other young men his age. One fellow, Al Collins, became Dad's prayer partner, and they attended church, studied, and prayed continually. One night Al had a dream in which he and Dad were on a large, solid rock surrounded by murky waters. He and Dad were fending off snakes by using a large rod in their hands. Suddenly Al's feet began slipping, and he said to Dad, "Fred, I left you on that rock to fight the battle. I went into the water and was taken under!" They both knew this was a warning of an impending satanic attack, but little did they realize that Al would be diagnosed with a brain tumor that months later would take his life.

After Al's death, Dad was sorrowful and was praying about entering the Korean War. He was alone, praying outside of a small one-roomed shack that the fellows had built for study and prayer. Leaning his chair back against the outside wall, Dad felt a hand grab his right shoulder through the wall! He suddenly slumped over and instantly felt his spirit depart his body, moving faster than the speed of light upward into the universe. He thought perhaps he had died of a heart attack. Dad described how he eventually stopped somewhere out in the universe and was surrounded by the most beautiful sapphire blue heaven. He was standing on nothing, but he felt no fear.

Suddenly he observed a silver ball of light approaching him in the far distance. To his amazement, Al Collins stepped from this light, raised his right hand, and said, "Fred, God has called you to preach." He lowered his hand, then lifting it a second time, he spoke, "Fred, God told me to tell you that you must preach." Without any warning, Al stepped back into the light and appeared to travel into the beautiful blue open space and disappear. Dad suddenly felt his spirit moving at a high speed as it reentered his body. (See 2 Corinthians

12:1–4.) When he came to himself in the chair, the hair on Dad's body was standing straight up. The energy he felt from the experience was *electrifying*! Dad gave his name to the draft board, but he was never called into the military!

There are some who do not believe the Lord could or would allow such an amazing incident to occur. However, consider the supernatural calling of Saul of Tarsus into the ministry. Saul was traveling to Damascus, Syria, with legal papers to arrest key Christian church leaders. Saul's journey was suddenly interrupted by a heavenly light, as Christ Himself spoke to Saul from heaven (Acts 9:3–5). The light was so brilliant that Saul became blind and had to be led into the city of Damascus (Acts 22:11). The calling from God came directly out of heaven and was verbally given by Christ Himself, who had died, been raised from the dead, and was positioned in heaven when He spoke to Saul and announced that Saul was a chosen vessel. While my father was certainly no Saul of Tarsus, his call into the ministry was dramatic and necessary, as he was preparing to enter the Korean War, which would have completely *disrupted the destiny of his future family*. In all likelihood, had he entered the Korean War, he would not have married my mother, and she would not have given birth to four children—including their preaching son who is writing this book!

In using this illustration, remember that according to the Scriptures, when we are absent from the body we are present with the Lord (2 Cor. 5:8), and our spirit departs our body at death (Matt. 27:50; Acts 5:5; 12:23). A righteous spirit will enter the third heaven in a dwelling place called *paradise* (2 Cor. 12:1–4). Thus, the righteous are not actually dead; their eternal spirits are very much alive and living in another realm.

I believe my father had an *out-of-body experience* similar to what Paul described when he saw the third heaven (2 Cor. 12:1–4). God allowed Dad to see his close friend, who confirmed to him that God's will was for Dad to preach. Please note: Dad did not ask or pray to see Al, but God permitted it in His sovereignty.

DYING SAINTS SEE DEAD SAINTS

Prior to the death of Christ, God sent two Old Testament prophets to speak with Him on the Mount of Transfiguration. These two great leaders, Elijah and Moses, appeared and discussed with Christ the events that would surround His death in Jerusalem (Luke 9:28–33). I cannot tell you the number of times that family members have told of their precious mother, dad, or grandparents who, just prior to death, began to see the family members who had gone on to be with the Lord. Many times a dying person will be physically weak with his or her eyes shut and suddenly will become fully alert and aware of all of the surroundings. Then, in a weak voice that person will say, "Let those young men through; they are coming for me," or ask, "Can't you see the angels in this room?" When a person in a hospital or at home who is expected to die begins seeing loved ones who have passed, it usually indicates that the person will shortly go to be with the Lord. When Stephen, the first martyr in the early church, was being stoned to death by the religious fanatics of his day, he said, "I see the heavens opened and the Son of man standing at the right hand of God!" (Acts 7:56). Stephen saw into the spirit world moments before he called upon the Lord to "receive [his] spirit" (v. 59). Moments before departing, his eyes were opened to see into the next dimension.

I have personally spoken with individuals who survived major surgery and saw (in a clear vision) loved ones who had passed on. What I am going to share now is very important. In every instance the only people to appear were those who were solid, praying people who loved the Lord. At times the person in the hospital would question where other family members were, but they never appeared. In each instance a believer never saw a person who died without Christ! In other words, in such situations those who died lost have never appeared to anyone to warn them about the land of lost souls. Why is this?

In Luke 16:19–31 Christ revealed a true story of a poor man who begged for food and a rich man who refused to feed him. Both men died. The poor man went to paradise, and the selfish rich man found his spirit in hell. The rich man begged that the poor man would come back from the dead and warn his five brothers not to come to this forbidden place. The answer to this tormented man's request was, "They have Moses and the prophets; let them hear [believe] them....If they do not hear [believe] Moses and the prophets, neither will they be persuaded though one rise from the dead" (vv. 29–31). The reason for this comment is that someone who believes in the Bible should also believe in the supernatural and the afterlife, which are taught about through the Scriptures. Sinners, agnostics, or unbelievers would never believe if they actually saw someone from the dead. They would tag it as a hallucination, a wild imagination, or a result of some medication they were on. This happens now when a believer tells the average doctor that he or she saw the afterlife or a loved one who had passed. An unbeliever is an unbeliever, and seeing a departed loved one will not change that.

Christ had to stop Saul on the road to Damascus, blind him in a light, show him a vision, and speak in an audible voice before this rebellious and stubborn Pharisee of Pharisees would pay any attention (Acts 9:1–8). Saul later revealed that those traveling with him that day saw the "light" but never heard the "voice" (Acts 22:9). Saul, whose name was later changed to Paul, called this incident a "heavenly vision" (Acts 26:19). Some saw a light and heard nothing. What

God allows you to see and hear can be based upon your personal level of spiritual commitment to Him.

One of my staff workers, Sherree Fister, recently lost her stepfather, Rev. Eugene Nicola, because of cancer. Days before he passed, he became quite weak. However, he also became very alert to the spirit world. He began telling the family, "I have seen the colors of heaven." He also said he could hear the music of heaven. After several unusual encounters when his eyes were opened to the next life, he told his family gathered near his bed, "I want to go on home because it's too carnal here!"

WHY GOD LETS YOU SEE A DEPARTED LOVED ONE

At times when a person dreams about a departed loved one, it *can be* a dream from the Lord. When seeing a vision, a person appears very clear and in a three-dimensional form. A vision can be so *real* that the person may seem to have returned from paradise to *literally* appear before you. In Stephen's vision Christ appeared and was standing in heaven. In John's apocalyptic vision, the seer was on the island of Patmos but was caught up "in the Spirit" to the heavenly temple (Rev. 1:10). The entire Book of Revelation is a vision of things to come.

Seeing a departed loved one appear to you on Earth may not necessarily indicate that person has actually left the paradise of the righteous souls in heaven and returned to Earth. God can permit a soul that is now in heaven to appear in a vision in the same manner Christ appeared to Saul on the road to Damascus. The question is this: Why would the Lord allow a person to see someone in a dream or a vision who has gone home to be with Him? I believe there are four possible reasons.

1. At times to bring you comfort

There are times when a person departs and the family members are uncertain of the spiritual condition of the departed. Perhaps they were raised in a church, confessed Christ at one point, but had not been as active for the kingdom as they should. On several occasions in the Bible the Lord allowed people who had died to appear and tell their family members that they were all right and not to worry about them. This does not mean that in every case we can ask for some type of confirmation and experience a dream or a vision of a person. For this to occur it must be the sovereign purpose of God, which is something none of us can manipulate or control.

2. To bring back positive memories

When a wonderful person who brought you joy is taken from you, it leaves you with only memories. These memories are like precious pictures that capture a moment in time on photo paper. From time to time we pull out numerous albums and laugh when we see how much we changed over the years. My wife always tells me I am much better-looking now, so needless to say, I love pulling those pictures out to remind her how blessed she is (bear with me in my folly)!

God can see when we are sad, lonely, or despondent. At times we may see a husband, wife, or a child in a dream who is now with Christ, and the wonderful memories resurface, bringing us joy and recharging all of the fun family memories that we keep hidden in our spirits.

3. To give you hope for the resurrection

One of the greatest comforts for a believer in Christ is the hope of the resurrection. This is the exciting hope that a believer has that when the dead in Christ are raised, we will be reunited with our dear friends and loved ones. This is perhaps the reason why, after many years, it seems as though my precious grandparents are still living—because they are in the paradise of God in heaven, where their spirits are waiting for the resurrection of the dead!

When we see them in a dream, we are reminded that one day the dream will become a reality at the return of Christ. We will see them again. Martha understood this when she reminded Christ that at the resurrection she would see her brother, Lazarus, again (John 11).

4. To give you a premonition of death

I want to be very careful in expressing and explaining this fourth reason, as it would be easy for someone to misunderstand a simple dream that may occur with a departed loved one in the dream. However, there have been times when an older saint would see godly family members appear in a dream to tell them it was getting time for them to come home. I remember that several months before my grandfather passed on, he called me and said, "I had an unusual dream. I fell asleep in my easy chair and saw my dad, my mother, and my little brother Tony, who died in the 1930s."

I asked him what he saw. He said, "They were telling me, 'Johnny, it's about time for you to come home.'" He had also seen a large mansion-like building in a dream that was located somewhere in heaven. He felt he was given a warning that he would soon pass away. He was in very good health for his age except for some minor heart problems.

My father and I were both given dreams about the same time involving Granddad. I dreamed I was standing in the bathroom of the old home place. Suddenly three of the four walls collapsed near the toilet. I was uncertain of what it meant, but it was the restroom Granddad always used that was next to his and my grandmother's bedroom. Dad then dreamed that Granddad was working in the attic and became twisted in wires. He fell among the wires and died.

Weeks later Granddad was taken to the Elkins Hospital for surgery on his intestines. After the surgery he had three strokes, affecting his brain, and he became like a vegetable, lying in the intensive care unit. It seemed as if wires were connected to every part of his body. This is where he passed away. The restroom and the toilet in my dream indicated the intestinal problem, and the three walls that fell were the three strokes he had that collapsed his body. The house with the attic was his body, and the attic his mind. He was hooked up to machines with various wires to monitor the heart, breathing, and brain activity, and he died hooked up to the equipment. The two dreams were actually the same from a slightly different perspective.

Please understand that a dream of a departed loved one does not mean you or anyone else near you is going to die. There can be numerous reasons, including no specific reason at all, why you have a dream.

DREAMING OF YOUR OWN DEATH

As parents, we are all concerned about our children, and often in our subconscious we find our minds musing on the numerous possibilities of what could bring harm to them, especially when they are infants or children too weak to defend themselves. We all know there are promises of angelic protection for our children (Matt. 18:10). This subconscious concern can lead to silent worry, which, in return, causes tormenting dreams that something terrible will happen to them.

Because my mother became pregnant at age forty, she was very protective of her little girl Melanie, as any mother would be. Mom said she would have tormenting dreams of something bad happening, but she realized this was the adversary causing her to fret. The same occurred after my son was born. I dreamed several times that he died as a child. Pam and I prayed each day (and continue to pray) that an angel of the Lord would protect our son and our daughter. When Jonathan was about four, we were staying in a hotel in Maryland. His mother was downstairs doing laundry, and I was in a room beside him where he was watching television. Pam came in and said, "Where's Jonathan?"

I relied, "He's in the next room." She walked through the door adjoining the rooms, and he was not there. We panicked! We went down the hall, listening to hear a child crying, and ended up at the elevator. We pressed the button, and there he was, all by himself. He said, "I want Mommy." He did not know the button to press inside the elevator. Anyone could have snatched him and left without us ever seeing him again.

As he grew, I knew we must trust the Lord to protect the family at home and in our journeys. The adversary will lay additional weight on your heart if fear is present. Then you will have tormenting dreams that haunt you throughout the day. Dreaming of a death of a child should cause you to check if there is a fear that needs to be dealt with or if it is a warning. Pray for protection and peace—both of which are promised in the Scriptures.

What if you dream of your own death? Secular dream researchers tell us that this may indicate a new beginning of a marriage or job. However, it can also be an indication of a fear of death. On rare occasions it may be a warning that you should pray, as prayer can change circumstances. Hezekiah was told he was going to die, but his crying and prayer reached God, and his life was extended fifteen additional years (2 Kings 20:6).

I was friends with a well-known Jewish rabbi from Jerusalem named Getz. The rabbi would go to his office every day in the late evening to pray, often until the early hours of the morning. He told his wife that the Lord came to him and told him that he was going to pass in two weeks. It happened exactly as he said.

It is noted that President Abraham Lincoln was given two dreams about his death. The first occurred before his 1860 election. In it he saw he saw two images of his own face in a mirror. One was very pale and disappeared when he looked at it.[1] Many believed it was a sign he would not survive his second term.

Abraham Lincoln wrote about a strange dream he had in March or April of 1865:

> I retired very late. I had been up waiting for important dispatches from the front. I could not have been long in bed when I fell into a slumber, for I was weary. I soon began to dream. There seemed to be death-like stillness about me. Then I heard subdued sobs, as if a number of people were weeping. I thought I left my bedroom and wandered downstairs. There the silence was broken by the same pitiful sobbing, but the mourners were invisible. I went from room to room; no living person was in sight, but the same mournful sounds of distress met me as I passed along. It was light in all of the rooms; every object was familiar to me; but where were all the people who were grieving as if their hearts would break? I was puzzled and alarmed. What could be the meaning of all of this? Determined to find the cause of a state of things so mysterious and so shocking, I kept on until I arrived at the East Room, which I entered. There I met with a sickening surprise. Before me was a catafalque, on which rested a corpse wrapped in funeral vestments. Around it were stationed soldiers who were acting as guards; and there was a throng of people, some gazing mournfully upon the corpse, whose face was covered, others weeping pitifully. "Who is dead in the White House?" I demanded of one of the soldiers. "The President," was his answer; "he was killed by an assassin!" Then came a loud burst of grief from the crowd, which awoke me from my dream.[2]

Two weeks later, on April 14, Lincoln was assassinated at Ford's Theatre by John Wilkes Booth. His casket was laid in the East Room, guarded by soldiers as seen in his dream!

It is reported that the very night before his assassination Lincoln informed a member of his cabinet about this dream. On the morning before his assassination, Lincoln told his bodyguard, W. H. Crook, about his dream, saying he had dreamed about the event three times. Crook begged the president not to go to the theatre that evening. Crook noted that before they left for the theatre, Lincoln, who normally said, "Good night," said to Crook, "Good-bye."[3]

This is a strong example of a well-known person dreaming (according to Crook) three times that he would die.

THE PREMONITION OF DEATH

People often speak of having a *premonition* of a future event, or a foreboding that something is going to happen. A *premonition* is an advance warning of something that is going to happen. This occurred when Elijah and the sons of the prophets were given a forewarning that the prophet Elijah was to be taken alive to heaven. Elisha was following Elijah to the towns of the sons of the prophets, who all knew Elijah was going to heaven that day:

> Now the sons of the prophets who were at Bethel came out to Elisha, and said to him, "Do you know that the LORD will take away your master from over you today?" And he said, "Yes, I know; keep silent!"
>
> —2 KINGS 2:3

At two locations, Bethel and Jericho, "sons of the prophets" were forewarned about the departure of the great prophet to occur on that day (2 Kings 2:1–6). The text indicates that Elijah was the first to know he would be taken in a whirlwind that day (v. 1). What is interesting is that Elijah was actually taken up in a *chariot with horses of fire*, which Elisha saw (vv. 11–12), but the sons of the prophets at Jericho only saw the physical *wind* and later requested a search party to look three days for Elijah's body (vv. 16–18). The men at Jericho saw the whirlwind, but Elisha saw the chariot of fire, which, to the natural eye, was invisible (v. 17). One man saw the invisible chariot and others saw only the wind. This indicates that godly people may be at different levels of spiritual perception. Some have greater spiritual insight and vision than others, and much of it comes through generational blessings (Elisha received a double portion of Elijah's anointing) and also through continual personal prayer.

I can count seven different occasions when I came under a very heavy burden—a strong foreboding that someone would soon pass. The inner weight I felt was a burden unlike any other I have experienced. I always inform my wife and my closest associates at work when this overwhelming sense of loss comes. At times the spiritual pressure in my heart becomes so strong I leave work and go home to meditate and pray. I am unable to enjoy anything or be around anyone, only with the Lord. Always, when this happens, a very close relative or friend passes away unexpectedly within seven days. I confess that when this gut-wrenching feeling suddenly overwhelms me, I do not treat it lightly. This is simply the Holy Spirit preparing me for the loss.

When you either dream of a death, including your own, or have a premonition that something is rising over the horizon, the single most significant act for you to engage in is intercessory prayer. When you are uncertain what or for whom to pray, the Holy Spirit "makes intercession for [you]"; He is sent to assist you in your personal prayer life (Rom. 8:26–28). As you pray, you may have a strong impression of a certain person, and your spiritual focus becomes that individual. This *can be* an indication of death for the one you are praying for, and your prayers could prevent a premature departure (Eccles. 7:17). On several occasions my father saw in a mental vision that something bad was going to happen. Each time he would enter his prayer room to intercede. Usually within twenty-four to forty-eight hours, we would know what his burden was about.

In my book *Angels on Assignment* I share a very dramatic incident in the life of my father and his brother Morgan. This illustrates the power of prayer to prevent a premature *death*.

> In the mid 1980s, Dad was in deep prayer and saw a vision of an accident. He clearly saw a coal truck hitting a vehicle head-on, and he saw that the person sitting on the passenger side had been decapitated. He sensed it was a warning for his brother Morgan, who lived in West Virginia. Dad went to the phone and attempted to call Morgan several times but to no avail. He told Mom, "I am going to the church to pray, and don't let anyone bother me under any circumstance." Dad described to me that he interceded under such a heavy prayer burden that his stomach muscles began to hurt. He was pleading with God to spare his brother's life.
>
> After one hour, he heard the Holy Spirit tell him, "Son, you are asking Me to spare the life of one who has known Me but willfully has chosen to turn from Me. He is not walking in covenant with Me." This caused Dad to pray even more intently for another thirty minutes, asking God to extend his mercy to Morgan. It was then that Dad heard the Holy Spirit speak to him again, saying, "When you pastored in Northern Virginia, I showed you an angel that would be with you when you needed him. If you will ask the Father to send your angel to protect your brother, He will do so." Dad began to ask the Lord to send a protective angel to wherever Morgan was at that time.

It was later that evening when Dad got Morgan on the phone and told him that he had prayed for him to be spared from death. Morgan related this story to Dad: That morning he and a friend had gone to town and were returning home in his truck. Morgan felt a strange urge to stop at a small restaurant and get a soda. Morgan's neighbors, who lived across the street, were following them in a car and passed them as Morgan's truck turned into the restaurant parking lot. A few minutes later, both men were on the road heading home. To their shock, as they rounded a curve a mile up the road, they discovered that a large coal truck had struck the car with the neighbors, killing them both and decapitating the woman passenger. Dad said, "Morgan, that was intended for you, but the Lord sent His angel to have you stop for a few minutes so you would not be on the path of that huge coal truck!" This incident brought Morgan into a restored relationship with the Lord.[4]

Whether you experience a vision, a dream, or a premonition, prayer is the key to understanding what is planned and, at times, to prevent a tragedy! The only way to know if a warning is changeable is by seeking the face of the Lord and asking Him to alter and change a dangerous situation or to protect those you have seen in the dream or vision from harm and danger. Again, I have witnessed this so many times in the life of my father, as he was warned about family members, church members, or other individuals and would spend hours in prayer petitioning God to prevent a tragedy or alter a situation.

THE LAW OF THE DOUBLE DREAM

And the dream was repeated to Pharaoh twice because the thing is established by God, and God will shortly bring it to pass.

« Genesis 41:32 »

This one passage found in the story of Joseph interpreting Pharaoh's dream presents a special nugget to the reader. The king of Egypt had dreamed two dreams the same night. We read:

> Then Pharaoh said to Joseph: "Behold, in my dream I stood on the bank of the river. Suddenly seven cows came up out of the river, fine looking and fat; and they fed in the meadow. Then behold, seven other cows came up after them, poor and very ugly and gaunt, such ugliness as I have never seen in all the land of Egypt. And the gaunt and ugly cows ate up the first seven, the fat cows. When they had eaten them up, no one would have known that they had eaten them, for they were just as ugly as at the beginning. So I awoke. Also I saw in my dream, and suddenly seven heads came up on one stalk, full and good. Then behold, seven heads, withered, thin, and blighted by the east wind, sprang up after them. And the thin heads devoured the seven good heads."
>
> —Genesis 41:17–24

These two dreams were dreamed back to back on the same night, with the king waking up for a brief time between the first and the second dream. It is clear that the skinny cattle and the thin stalks of grain devouring the good cows and grain both deal with the same event—a famine. However, one truth about a spiritual dream that Joseph revealed should be noted: dreaming the same dream twice the same night can be an indicator that the dream is certain and will come to pass (Gen. 41:25, 32).

There is another *double* principle in the Scripture—when God calls a person's name twice. Normally we read, "And the LORD said to Abraham..." (Gen. 18:13), or "The LORD spoke to Moses..." (Exod. 6:10), or "The LORD said to Solomon..." (1 Kings 11:11). When addressing or appearing before a person in most references, the Scripture indicates that the Lord spoke their name *once*. However, there are several occasions in which the Almighty spoke the person's name *twice*. We read:

> But the Angel of the LORD called to him from heaven and said, "Abraham, Abraham!" So he said, "Here I am."
>
> —GENESIS 22:11

> Now the LORD came and stood and called as at other times, "Samuel, Samuel!" And Samuel answered, "Speak, for Your servant hears."
>
> —1 SAMUEL 3:10

> And the Lord said, "Simon, Simon! Indeed, Satan has asked for you, that he may sift you as wheat."
>
> —LUKE 22:31

> Then he fell to the ground, and heard a voice saying to him, "Saul, Saul, why are you persecuting Me?"
>
> —ACTS 9:4

God called these names twice to seize the attention of the individual. The purpose was to indicate to that person that a major *transition* or *change* was in the process. God called Abraham's name twice to prevent him from offering his son on the altar. With Samuel, he was a young boy, and God was preparing to transfer the office of the priesthood in Israel from Eli's house to Samuel. The lad would become the future spiritual adviser for Israel's first and second kings, Saul and David. Simon's name had been changed to Peter by Christ Himself (Matt. 16:17–18). However, in Luke 22:13, Christ used his former name, Simon, and spoke it twice. The Lord warned Peter that Satan was setting a strategy against him, determining to shake Peter's faith. The fourth example where God said, "Saul, Saul," is where the proud Pharisee from Jerusalem was, at that very moment, receiving a heavenly visitation from Christ, which led to his conversion while on the road to Damascus. Saul's name was then changed to Paul (Acts 13:9).

Just as the *double name* caught the attention of the person addressed, so a double dream on the same night is an indicator that the dream is established from the Lord and will come to pass in a short time. Many years ago in my earlier ministry I had a very troubling dream involving serpents. During the first dream the symbolism indicated that some form of difficulty (actually a spiritual attack) would follow a revival at a local church. This dream was immediately followed up by a second dream about a serpent in which the snake bit my feet and then rose up and bit my forehead. I knew the feet represented carrying the gospel (Rom. 10:15), and my head represented my thought life. Needless to say, I was very concerned about these two warnings, as serpents in a dream always represent great difficulty in the form of a trial.

Several months later, the very symbolism I saw in those dreams, which indicated a sudden trial, actually unfolded at a local church. The repercussion of that event was so intense at that season that I fought one of the most difficult mental battles of my ministry. One part I remembered in the first dream helped to sustain me through the entire trial. In the dream, when the serpent bit me in the feet and the head, I heard an audible voice say, "The serpent will bite you, but it will not kill you!" In the midst of the fiery trial, these words continually echoed in my mind. Somehow I would survive and even defeat the attack in the end. That is exactly what occurred.

WHY DOUBLE?

Many believers have experienced a dream that later came to pass, and yet they did not dream the same images twice. Just because you have a spiritual visitation and it does not occur twice does not mean the single dream is not from the Lord or that it will not come to pass. However, there may be a deeper reason as to why a dream is doubled.

There is a biblical principle concerning the power of agreement that is linked with the number two. Christ selected twelve disciples (Luke 9:1). However, He divided a team of seventy ministers into thirty-five teams of two each and commissioned them to teach and pray for the needs of the sick in every community (Luke 10:1). There has been speculation as to the purpose of having two disciples on each team. The writer in Ecclesiastes gave insight when he wrote:

> Two are better than one,
> Because they have a good reward for their labor.
> For if they fall, one will lift up his companion.
> But woe to him who is alone when he falls,
> For he has no one to help him up.
> Again, if two lie down together, they will keep warm;
> But how can one be warm alone?
> Though one may be overpowered by another, two can
>   withstand him.
> And a threefold cord is not quickly broken.
>   —ECCLESIASTES 4:9–12

There is a certain level of strength that multiplies when one person joins with another. Spiritual authority is increased when two join together in agreement. Christ said:

> Assuredly, I say to you, whatever you bind on earth will
> be bound in heaven, and whatever you loose on earth will
> be loosed in heaven. Again I say to you that if two of you
> agree on earth concerning anything that they ask, it will
> be done for them by My Father in heaven. For where two

or three are gathered together in My name, I am there in the midst of them.

—MATTHEW 18:18–20

This authority is not released just because two people are in the same room. They must *agree* as to what they believe God for. The Greek word for "agree" is *sumphoneo*, and it means to be in harmony, or, in this instance, to say the same thing. For example: When a church is informed that a fellow member is in critical condition in the hospital, and they are asked to pray, some may stand and petition the Lord with this prayer: "Father, may Your will be done…" A second group may be praying, "Lord, help him somehow…" The third group may sense faith and request, "Lord, enter that room and raise him from his deathbed…" A final circle of saints may be actually praying, "God, he's lived a long life. Don't let him suffer, and take him on if You see fit…" This is what I call a *hit-or-miss* prayer, or a *shooting-from-the-lip* prayer! There is only unity when the group is asking for the same thing. In this illustration there are four different types of prayers being offered, with no single *agreement* among the whole congregation. Perhaps this is why there is a lack of seeing congregational prayers answered; there are too many arrows being shot in different directions, and none are hitting their mark!

The authority is released when two people agree. The same is true with the manifest presence of the Lord. When two or three are "gathered together," Christ is in their midst. Throughout the world, on any given occasion there may be two or three believers in the same room—and no particular presence of Christ can be felt. So is this verse untrue? No, because the key is in the words "gathered together," which is more than just meeting in one place; it alludes to being *led* to the same place. When you are led by the Holy Spirit as you gather, then the Lord is in your midst. All it takes is at least two to agree or be led together in one place!

Just as revealed by Christ, the law of God established the need for two witnesses in any judicial case involving manslaughter. One witness alone could not condemn a person, for it is written, "Whoever kills a person, the murderer shall be put to death on the testimony of witnesses; but one witness is not sufficient testimony against a person for the death penalty" (Num 35:30). We read, "Whoever is deserving of death shall be put to death on the testimony of two or three witnesses; he shall not be put to death on the testimony of one witness" (Deut. 17:6). Moses taught the people that in the mouth of two or three witnesses every word would be established (Deut. 19:15).

The necessity of at least two verbal statements to establish a fact comes into play when we understand that Pharaoh had the dream, but a second person, Joseph, interpreted the meaning. Thus there were two men led together in an inspired moment that would save Egypt and set the destiny for the nation of Israel. The double dream is similar to two witnesses who can establish a fact. When a dream is doubled, it means it is confirmed to come to pass.

Personally, I don't recall speaking to many believers who have dreamed the same dream twice. It is certainly a rare occurrence, but a person should give heed to the dream and understand there is a spiritual precedent about dreaming twice.

eleven

ANGEL APPEARANCES IN DREAMS

Then he dreamed, and behold, a ladder was set up on the earth, and its top reached to heaven; and there the angels of God were ascending and descending upon it.

« Genesis 28:12 »

What visual impression do you experience when a person says "an angel of the Lord"? As a child, I would visualize a tall supernatural being that looked somewhat like a man with huge golden wings connected to his shoulders and blond hair the color of gold. His face was glowing and radiating like the noonday sun. Throughout the Scriptures, there were numerous appearances of angels. However, there are very few references that give a detailed description as to what their appearance is like. In many instances the appearance is based upon the type of angel each scripture is speaking of.

For example, the prophet Daniel was fasting for three weeks to receive the understanding of a very complicated vision he had experienced. After twenty-one days, an angel of the Lord appeared to him and gave him a lengthy, detailed interpretation, revealing many events linked to the time of the end. (See Daniel 10–12.) Here is the description of the "man" Daniel saw:

> Now on the twenty-fourth day of the first month, as I was by the side of the great river, that is, the Tigris, I lifted my eyes and looked, and behold, a certain man clothed in linen, whose waist was girded with gold of Uphaz! His body was like beryl, his face like the appearance of lightning, his eyes like torches of fire, his arms and feet like burnished bronze in color, and the sound of his words like the voice of a multitude. And I, Daniel, alone saw the vision, for the men who were with me did not see the vision; but a great terror fell upon them, so that they fled to hide themselves.
>
> —Daniel 10:4–7

This male being, an angel, was clothed in linen, which is the same material worn by the seven angels in the Book of Revelation (Rev.

15:6), and is the same white cloth remnant worn by the saints at the marriage supper of the Lamb in Revelation 19:8. The white linen represents "righteousness" (Rev. 19:8). This angel wore a golden belt, which is similar in description to the golden belt (girdle) worn by Christ Himself in John's vision (Rev. 1:13). The description of this angel's body is interesting; it was identified as appearing like beryl. Pure beryl is colorless, but beryl with impurities can appear with a greenish, greenish-blue, or yellow color. The greenish-colored beryl is similar to that of an emerald. The streets in heaven are gold, but transparent gold (Rev. 21:21). Even twenty-four-karat gold is not transparent. The gold in heaven must have a level of purity that is unknown on Earth. If pure beryl is colorless and has the appearance of a crystal, then this angel may have had a translucent, glassy-like color, almost like a hologram, with some slight form of color that reminded Daniel of a beryl stone—a greenish-yellow gold type of appearance. This is significant, since angels are *spirits*, and spirits cannot be seen with the natural eyes.

The face of this angel was shining as the sun, which is also the same imagery painted by John when he saw Christ in the vision recorded in Revelation 1:16. The eyes of the angel were like "torches of fire." In ancient times, oil lamps were used to bring light into a building at night. When burning, an oil lamp forms a flame that can be similar to the shape of human eyes. Christ is also identified in Revelation with "eyes like a flame of fire" (v. 14). The body, arms, and feet of the angel in Daniel's vision were similar to polished brass. The same words are used to identify Christ, when John wrote that "His feet were like fine brass, as if refined in a furnace" (v. 15). When brass is taken from the earth, it has a mix of copper and zinc; thus it only becomes a bright yellow-gold color after being refined in fire. The imagery here is that the angel had a very reflective, yellow-gold appearance. When the angel spoke, his voice sounded like a multitude of voices combined at once. Once again, John used similar words to describe Christ when he wrote, "And His voice as the sound of many waters" (v. 15).

Theologians have noted the similarities between this unnamed angel in Daniel and the appearance of Christ to John in Revelation 1. They identify the Daniel vision as a *theophany*, which is a Greek word meaning "appearance of God." In Christian and Jewish thought, a theophany is "any direct, visual manifestation of the presence of God." It would include the occasions in the Bible when God manifested Himself to men. Some theologians believe the angel in Daniel's vision was actually Christ Himself appearing to Daniel. The difficulty with this theory is that a demonic prince of Persia restrained this angel of the Lord for twenty-one days, and God assigned a mighty archangel named Michael to assist this angel, providing him the ability to be released from his warfare and appear to Daniel. I cannot see the preincarnate Christ as being hindered by any demonic spirit! However, angels do battle in the heavens with evil forces. (See Daniel 10 and Revelation 12:7–10.) This is only one description of an angel.

We know that angelic beings can appear in the form of light and fire. On two occasions the prophet Elisha saw "horses and chariots of fire." The first encounter was when his teacher, Elijah, was transported into heaven on a chariot of fire, driven by spirit horses that also manifested in the form of fire (2 Kings 2). When the Assyrian army was preparing to capture him, Elisha also saw a circle of protection around him and his servant. Elisha saw "horses and chariots of fire" (2 Kings 6:17).

When men like Ezekiel, Daniel, and John saw visions of heaven, they identified numerous types of angels, such as cherubim, seraphim, and living creatures. (See Ezekiel 1; Isaiah 6:1–3; Revelation 5.) These angels are beings that minister before the throne of God on a consistent and eternal basis, and their description of color of brass, many wings and many eyes, and the appearance of an eagle, lion, and man are both amazing and almost difficult to comprehend. However, when ministering angels appear in dreams, visions, or on Earth with a warning or instruction, they seldom appear in these higher-level forms.

ANGELS AS MEN IN DREAMS

Throughout especially the Old Testament, angels would appear to the patriarchs and the prophets in the form of men. These appearances were at times in visible human form and at other times in dreams or visions. In the time of Abraham, the Lord and two angels paid a visit to the tent of Abraham, where they ate with him and the Lord entered into a negotiation with Abraham concerning the city of Sodom. After the final agreement was sealed, the two angels traveled to Sodom and were mistaken for two men. Obviously they were not wearing white linen and did not have two golden wings. They had a flesh tone very similar to that of human men. In the Book of Hebrews, the writer informs the reader that we should be careful when entertaining strangers, for we may be unaware that they are angels (Heb. 13:2).

In a spiritual dream, an angel can appear in the form of a man. In one major experience in 1988, which remains with me to this day, I was given a direct instruction in a dream related to the future of my ministry. I was preaching in a tent in Leeds, Alabama, in a revival that had extended into its fourth week. Early in the morning, while in a deep sleep, I entered into a dream/night vision, which was very clear and vivid. I walked up a hill, crossed a paved road, and saw a set of concrete steps. I observed television towers with satellite dishes attached, and a man with an olive complexion and beautiful white hair, who stood about six feet four inches and was dressed in a black suit, was standing beside the television tower. He said to me, "Son, if you obey the Lord, God is going to give you this." Then he proceeded to give me three direct instructions from the Lord that required my obedience if I was to receive the fullness of God's blessing and minister to the world on television. At the time I did not own a television camera, did not have a studio, and knew nothing about a television ministry.

When I came out from under the influence of this dream/night vision, I was fully alert and awake and recalled every detail of what I saw. I told my wife and the head of my board of directors, Richard Towe. Rick replied, "The Lord has already spoken to my spirit that you will have a major television program in the future!" This was a confirmation.

When I told my father of this marvelous experience, I asked him, "Dad, who do you think the man was who was speaking to me?"

He replied, "That's obvious." He continued, "First, he called you 'son.' I am your earthly father, but God calls all men who are believers His sons. Because this man brought you a direct message from the Lord, he was a divine messenger, or an angel of the Lord."

I said, "I always thought that if an angel appeared in a dream, he would be in a white robe, with a gold tone, and maybe with a few wings." Dad reminded me of the angels that came to Sodom and the angel that wrestled with Jacob, who was described as: "a Man wrestled with him…" However, this "man" was actually an angel (Gen. 32:24–30). In fact, afterward, Jacob confessed that he had "seen God face to face" and lived through the experience (v. 30)!

Dad also noted that throughout his ministry, when the Lord gave him a spiritual dream or a vision, whenever the man in the dream would address him as "My son" or as "son" or "My servant," that the person in the dream/vision was a messenger from the Lord or an angel of the Lord.

This significant *nugget* from my wise father, Fred Stone, has been a great help to me over the years when I dream and see a man that may appear as just another person, but the dream or vision has biblical symbolism and imagery and the person is bringing a message from the Lord.

The Book of Ezekiel is a major prophetic book with warnings and apocalyptic overtones throughout the book. Ezekiel witnessed the heavens open and saw four living creatures carrying the throne of God throughout the earth (Ezek. 1). He experienced the vision of the dry bones (Ezek. 37), the war of Gog and Magog (Ezek. 38–39), and the future millennial temple in Jerusalem (Ezek. 40–48). The Lord appeared to Ezekiel and called him "son of man" ninety-three times in the Book of Ezekiel!

Under the redemptive covenant, believers are called "sons of God" (John 1:12, KJV; 1 John 3:2, KJV).

I truly believe that one of the reasons that the Lord allows an angel to appear in the form of a normal-looking man in a dream is because the mental, physical, and spiritual responses we would encounter if the Lord showed us the full glory of the cherubim, seraphim, or the living creatures would be too overwhelming for us to handle. When men saw angels in their fullness in the Bible, they fell to the ground! In Daniel 10, when Daniel saw the angel, he was on his face toward the ground. The other men with him saw nothing, but they also began trembling and fled from the scene (Dan. 10:7–9). Abraham fell on his face when he heard the voice of God (Gen. 17:3). Joshua fell down when he saw the "Commander of the army of the LORD" near Jericho (Josh. 5:14). Even the donkey of Balaam fell down at the presence of an angel (Num. 22:27). During John's vision of the resurrected Christ, he "fell at His feet as dead" (Rev. 1:17).

Seeing any angel in a full-color, three-dimensional vision causes trembling, fear, and a physical response. I have experienced *nightmares* where I woke up feeling like my heart was beating out of my chest. If the Lord allowed us to see the full glory of an angel in an open or night vision, many of us could not take it! We would suffer from a heart attack! This is why I suggest that God will send an angel in human form to prevent the *shock* the human mind and body could experience if we were to see the full manifestation and the total glory of the realm of heaven and the world of spirits.

ANGELS WITH NEW REVELATIONS

If you experience a dream in which the Lord calls you a son or daughter and an *angel* brings you a message from the Lord, always remember that messages from heaven will always agree with the Holy Scriptures. I am an avid reader of all types of books, news articles, and commentaries. I recall reading a lengthy article months ago in which a noted *Christian seer* was claiming visitations from an angel that was giving her important information from varied "heavenly sources." There was a major problem, however, because her "messages" indicated that there were other sources of redemption outside of Jesus Christ. She was actually preaching the traditions that can be found among some who claim that there is a secondary source of intercession and forgiveness of sins besides Christ. At this point, any alleged messenger is not from the Lord. This is why Paul wrote:

> But even if we, or an angel from heaven, preach any other gospel to you than what we have preached to you, let him be accursed. As we have said before, so now I say again, if anyone preaches any other gospel to you than what you have received, let him be accursed.
>
> —Galatians 1:8–9

There are two well-known and quite popular religions that are based upon the founder allegedly receiving messages and revelations from angels, including the angel Gabriel. I have studied both of these religions and their beliefs, and the alleged angel totally contradicted the inspired Word of God. In one case the founder reported that Gabriel revealed to him that God has no son and that Jesus is not the Son of God. Of course we read in Luke's account that Gabriel told the Virgin Mary that the child in her womb would be "called the Son of God" (Luke 1:35). Therefore, the real Gabriel is not going to change his mind and bring a new revelation more than six hundred years after the conception of Christ! The woman *seer* and others like her are claiming to channel angel spirits. Those unfamiliar or ignorant of the Scriptures could fall prey to a false doctrine—and even dangerous heresy—by believing there are other sources of redemption, including even *co-redeemers* outside of Christ. The Bible is clear: "Nor is there salvation in any other, for there is no other name under heaven given among men by which we must be saved" (Acts 4:12).

In a dream or vision an angel of the Lord can bring you certain instructions or directions, but a true heavenly visitor will never contradict the revelation of Scripture. If the message causes divisions, turns men from Christ, and introduces other forms of redemption, it is a counterfeit angel of light. Paul warns against such a thing in 2 Corinthians 11:13–15:

> For such are false apostles, deceitful workers, transforming themselves into apostles of Christ. And no wonder! For Satan himself transforms himself into an angel of light. Therefore it is no great thing if his ministers also transform themselves into ministers of righteousness, whose end will be according to their works.

CAN ANGELS APPEAR AS WOMEN IN DREAMS?

On several occasions there have been very godly and biblically sound believers who have testified to receiving an important, personal word from the Lord in a dream in which the person was an angel of the Lord but appeared more in the form of a female than a male. In the past I would question why this was so or think that the person perhaps misread what he or she saw. However, after searching the Bible, I was quite amazed to read a unique passage written by the prophet Zechariah describing angels with female appearance:

> Then I raised my eyes and looked, and there were two women, coming with the wind in their wings; for they had wings like the wings of a stork, and they lifted up the basket between earth and heaven.
>
> —ZECHARIAH 5:9

When reading this, I first examined the word *women,* which does appear in the Hebrew text. The word is *ishshah,* a feminine word used for a woman or a female. The prophet indicated that these two "women" had wings like a stork. Some commentators mention that the stork is an unclean bird (Lev. 11:19), thus these two angelic-like figures are actually symbols of evil in the land of Shinar. I suggest that the prophet is simply attempting to identify how the wings looked when he saw these two lift up the lead basket and carry it into the land of Shinar. A stork has long wings attached to its back. This is the imagery the prophet is painting. These two women also have the wind in their wings. While some suggest this phrase is a metaphor, we do know from the Bible that during the Tribulation angels are seen "holding the four winds of the earth" (Rev. 7:1).

When suggesting that there are possibly angels in heaven that have the appearance of women, the first reaction is remembering that when Christ was asked about the resurrection of the dead and marriage in heaven, He replied, "For when they rise from the dead, they neither marry nor are given in marriage, but are like angels in heaven" (Mark 12:25–26). When studying the Bible, there are scriptures that reveal a direct and clear truth, and there are other times when certain truths can be *deduced* from the verse and the implications of what was being said. For example, when the Bible says that everyone will "receive a mark on their right hand or on their foreheads, and that no one may buy or sell except one who has the mark" (Rev. 13:16–17), this passage does not tell you what the mark is or how it can impact the ability of the entire world's population to purchase and sell. However, with computers and identification technology, we can see how this verse could come to pass.

When asked about marriage in heaven, why didn't Christ say, "Of course there is no marriage in heaven, as all of the angels are male, and therefore there are no females to marry." Instead He said, "They are like the angels, neither marrying or being given in marriage." The verse is silent, yet the *implication* is that there is a possibility of both male and female angelic beings in heaven. However, there is no marriage among the angels in heaven.

If these two women carrying the basket are female in gender, and the Hebrew word indicates they are, and they are *wicked spirits* and not angels of the Lord, then this would indicate female spirits in the satanic realm. If Satan's kingdom consists of fallen angels, and these two women are fallen angels, then their appearance would be like that of the angels before the wicked angels were cast out of heaven with Satan.

Perhaps the least controversial manner of interpreting this, according to some scholars, is to say that they appeared to the prophet to look like women but were not women. This is similar to the strange demonic locusts that come from the abyss during the Tribulation and had "faces of men" and "hair like women's hair"

(Rev. 9:7–8). In ancient cultures, women grew very long hair. Thus John described either the hairlike appearance or the headdress on these creatures as the appearance of women's hair. If these women simply had long hair and feminine-looking faces, then the argument is that all angels in Scripture are masculine in *appearance* except these two.

However, in most spiritual dreams and visions the messenger will appear in a masculine form. It is possible that God could permit an angel to appear as a woman in a dream, but this is certainly a very rare instance. Perhaps the controversy is better settled when we get to heaven!

It is certainly possible that a believer can experience a dream or vision in which the angel of the Lord appears in bright clothing and in a glorified form. At times, prior to a believer's departure from this life, some will speak of seeing either departed loved ones or a heavenly, angelic-like being just prior to their death. This is not uncommon, as Scripture indicates that angels are assigned to help a believer depart from their physical body at death. In Luke 16, when the poor beggar died, he was carried by the angels into the paradise of God, known in that time as "Abraham's bosom" (Luke 16:22). In these instances the appearance of an angel is often described as a glowing being in a white garment, standing in a room or near the bed. Whether the dying soul is actually seeing the angel or is having a true *open vision* is known only to the Lord. The fact is, angels have appeared and do appear in dreams, as indicated in both Testaments!

In summary:

▶ God can allow an angelic messenger to appear in a dream or a vision.

▶ The angel will more often appear in the form of a man and rarely, but occasionally, a woman.

► The angel will often address you as a son or daughter when speaking.

► The angel will inform you that the message has come for you from the Lord.

► The message will also agree with the Word of God.

I wish to make it clear that biblically we are not to be involved in angel worship or seeking angels. God's angelic messengers are commissioned into ministry activity by the voice of God Himself, and they respond only to the Word of God (Ps. 103:20). Any appearance of an angelic-type visitor in a dream, vision, or possible appearance in *human form* is completely controlled by the sovereignty of the Almighty and based upon the covenant of His Word.

twelve

WHY THE SYMBOLISM— CAN'T GOD MAKE IT PLAIN?

Pharaoh had a dream; and behold, he stood by the river. Suddenly there came up out of the river seven cows, fine looking and fat; and they fed in the meadow. Then behold, seven other cows came up out of the river, ugly and gaunt, and stood by the other cows on the bank of the river. And the ugly and gaunt cows at up the fine looking and fat cows.

So Pharaoh awoke.

« Genesis 41:1–4 »

One aspect of my ministry is the teaching of biblical prophecy. Today, more and more people are becoming aware of the ancient dreams and visions of the biblical prophets and are poring over the pages of the Holy Bible to unlock the cryptic codes and strange passages that have stumped scholars in previous generations. When I ask why a believer does not study or even read the apocalyptic books of the Scriptures, there always seems to be one main answer: "I don't understand all of the symbolism used, so I don't study it." The same is true with a real spiritual dream.

Oddly, most spiritual dreams that have instruction, warning, or important insight are often slightly veiled in symbolism. Many people who have experienced a spiritual dream may write the event off as some type of weird result of eating too much pizza before retiring for the night. Just as some folks can be slightly spiritually lazy when it comes to digging through the prophetic symbols to discover the dynamic insights, some believers have the attitude, "Well, if God wants to show me something, He can just show me!" This brings up a good point: Why can't the Lord just show you what is going to happen without using all of the strange symbolism often accompanying a spiritual dream? I believe I have found an answer.

First, most people dream throughout the night. In most dreams we are with friends or family and others we know, perhaps on a journey, in a church service, or on vacation, and it's just a *normal dream.* Then one night you have a dream that is quite different from the others. In this dream you see dark clouds slowly crawling in the sky toward your house. As you approach the door, there is a large snake lying in the entrance, looking for a way to get in. You see a sword and attack the serpent until he is dead, and then you enter. When you wake up, you know this was not a normal dream. You realize that in the Bible a serpent is Satan (or an enemy), and the door is the entrance to your home. A sword in Scripture is the "word of God" (Heb. 4:12), and you took a sword (the Word) to attack an enemy trying to get into your home! Thus, the symbolism was interpreted by using the Bible, and the dream is a warning of someone or something trying to get through the entrance of your home. You will need to fight it by the spoken Word of God!

The point is, without the symbolism it would be difficult to know if your dreams were just dreams or a dream from God! When Pharaoh dreamed, he saw seven good cows and seven lean cows, and seven good ears of corn and seven bad ears of corn near the Nile River. Cows eat grain and need water. Without grain and water, the cows become lean or die. The grain needs water to grow; without water, the grain will wither. The interpretation is clear; there was coming a lack of rain, leading to a famine. Grain was planted on a yearly cycle, thus seven stalks is a seven-year cycle. Joseph understood this to be a famine with a seven-year cycle. How else would God warn the king? The symbolism troubled Pharaoh and caused him to search out a man capable of the interpretation. Had it been just a simple dream, Pharaoh's own wise men could have revealed the meaning, and Joseph would had stayed in prison!

The same was true with Daniel. King Nebuchadnezzar dreamed of a metallic image that looked like a man. The head was gold, the chest and arms were of silver, the thighs were brass, the two legs were iron, and the two feet and ten toes were a mixture of iron and clay. (See Daniel 2.) The king was so troubled that he could not remember the dream. Daniel was called, and he not only revealed the dream, but he also gave the meaning, revealing that the various metals were different empires that would rule in succession of one another. How did Daniel know this was the meaning?

In Daniel's time, there was a belief among the Persians (Babylon's next-door neighbors) that the world empires were similar to a man with seven different kinds of metals. Although he did not understand the meaning of his dream, Nebuchadnezzar would also have been aware of this Persian belief. Babylon (the head of gold) had amassed huge amounts of gold, including the gold from the temple in Jerusalem. The Persians (represented by the silver chest and arms) raised tax money in silver coinage. Some even had silver harnesses for their horses. Since Greece and Rome were in the future, it would have been impossible for Daniel to give the meaning without the inspiration of the Lord upon him!

In the apocalyptic visions recorded in the Book of Daniel, even animals are used and identified with certain empires. I often wonder why certain animals were chosen to represent various empires. However, in my study I came to a conclusion that these were images that were already in existence and known among the ancients. For example, the ancient and modern empires all have animal-like symbols that are used to represent their particular empires, which are the same images found in the heavens. Daniel chapters 7 and 8 speak of a lion, a ram, and a goat.

Emblem	Empire	Heavenly Symbol	Parallel Emblem
Lion	Babylon	Lion emblem in heaven	Leo
Ram	Media-Persia	Ram emblem in heaven	Aries
Goat	Greece	Goat emblem in heaven	Capricorn
Eagle	Rome/America/Russia	Eagle emblem in heaven	Aquila
Dragon	China	Dragon emblem in heaven	Draco
Bear	Modern Russia	Bear emblem in heaven	Ursa Major

SIMPLE DREAM—COMPLICATED DREAMS

Some significant dreams are very plain, and others are veiled in symbolism. When my father was a teenager, the Korean War had broken out, and many young men from West Virginia were inducted into the army. The military had reported that two young men from the area of Bartley, West Virginia—namely, C. N. Morgan and Dale Smith—were missing and assumed killed in battle. The army was willing to pay death benefits to the parents. The mother of one soldier was a strong Christian and a faithful member of the church Dad was attending in Atwell, West Virginia. She requested prayer one evening, saying, "I don't believe my son is dead, and I want the saints to agree with me that God will find him and bring him home to me!" Some believers suggested that she was in denial, while others stood in faith with her.

Shortly thereafter Dad had a dream in which he saw both young men in very poor conditions, imprisoned in a North Korean prison camp. He saw Dale Smith standing deep in mud, holding onto a section of barbed wire. In the dream Smith spoke and said, "Brother Fred, please tell my mother that I am alive and being held as a prisoner in this camp. If she and the saints will pray, God is going to release us and bring us home safe." Dad immediately contacted the mother, informing her that both soldiers were alive, but that prayer was needed to bring about their releases! Some of the older believers felt that Dad was giving the mother false hope and that the dream was a smoke screen for a vivid and hopeful imagination. Others received the word and began continual intercession for their release.

Six months later Dad returned home from preaching a revival. When he stepped off the bus, his eye caught the local newspaper with the headlines, "Two Men Exchanged in Panmunjom Prisoner Swap." The writer reported that there had been a prisoner exchange between the United States and North Korea, and these two missing

West Virginia men were being released as part of the exchange. Needless to say, there was, as old-timers used to say, a *high time in Zion* when the news spread throughout the church!

This dream was a simple dream with a clear meaning. The men were missing but held in a camp. If the believers prayed, they would be released. There was no symbolism, simply a message with a meaning.

Many years later Dad was in his early thirties when his youngest brother, Lewis Stone, was ordered to Vietnam. I can remember hearing Dad pray for Lewis, and he always had him in his heart. One night in the month of December, Dad lay down in the bedroom to sleep. As he was dozing off, he was suddenly awakened by light coming into the room through a window located on the side of the driveway. He assumed that a car was turning around, when instantly he heard a voice say, "Lie down, I want to show you something." As he obeyed the voice, he immediately experienced a full-color vision. He was taken either in his mind or in the spirit to Vietnam. There he saw a group of marines digging a trench for the evening. In front of them was a field with tall grass. At the edge of the field were several trees. Dad saw three serpents crawling on the ground with rifles strapped to their backs; two had knives in their mouths. They were slowly crawling toward the marines, and Dad knew this was an unseen ambush. Dad marked the surroundings and suddenly came out of the vision with his heart pounding.

Not knowing what to do with the information, he sat down and penned a letter to Lewis, giving him the details of the planned ambush, including the site information, the three trees, and all other details he could remember. Dad sent the letter, praying that God would allow Lewis to get it in time. Many weeks later Dad heard back from Lewis, and the opening words were, "Fred...your dream was a true one..." He went on to describe the day they were digging in, how an ambush was set, and that the point man was shot to death. Out of eight hundred men who went into Vietnam with Lewis's company, only eight returned—Lewis Stone was one of those eight.

Other dreams or visions are veiled in symbolism. Years ago while touring Rome, Italy, I pondered as to why the Book of Revelation was written with so much symbolism. It occurred to me that chapters 17 and 18 speak of mystery Babylon's destruction—the city ruling over the kings of the earth. This is believed by many scholars to be a cryptic reference to the city of Rome, which was the headquarters of the Roman Empire in John's day. If John was predicting the total destruction of Rome and using the symbolism of Babylon to conceal the meaning, then it is clear why God chose the symbol of a woman riding a beast. If John would have clearly stated that the great city of Rome would be judged and destroyed in the future, then the Roman government, which had confined him to the desolate island of Patmos (Rev. 1:9), would have refused to allow John to bring the apocalyptic scroll with him when he was released from his captivity. John's prophecy of Rome's demise would have been considered to be anti-Roman propaganda. The Book of Revelation would have been confiscated and destroyed, never to be read in any church.

Imagine when John's Roman captors asked to see his writing, and they read of a flying red dragon, a women with a crown of twelve stars who was giving birth in heaven, and a woman hanging on to a ten-horned beast. Perhaps they would have thought, "This old man has been in the cave too long and needs some fresh air!" The bizarre symbolism may have actually provided protection for the actual scroll, allowing it to be copied and read throughout the first-century church.

While at times it may be challenging to the average believer to know if a dream is a natural or spiritual dream, there are several important guidelines to determine this difference that I have used during years of ministry. First, many *natural* or carnal dreams have no particular order and jump from scene to scene, person to person, or circumstance to circumstance. On the other hand, a spiritual dream usually has some form of order or progression to it. A spiritual dream will also have symbolism, which was also used in both the Old and New Testaments. As one example, a serpent throughout the Scriptures is a reference to Satan or an adversary of some form.

BIBLICAL SYMBOLISM AND PATTERNS

In the principles of biblical interpretation there is what is termed the "law of first mention." This hermeneutical principle states that when an object, number, color, or symbol is first mentioned in Scripture, then that sets the pattern for that object, number, color, or symbol throughout the Bible. Let's begin with certain biblical numbers.

The number four appears in Genesis when God created the sun, moon, and stars on the fourth day (Gen. 1:16–19). Afterward, it is mentioned when Moses wrote that there were four rivers that encompassed the Garden of Eden (Gen. 2:10). We later discover there are four directions on the earth: north, south, east, and west. Thus, from the onset of Scripture, the number four is an earthly number. Four Gospels reveal the earthly ministry of Jesus. The four living creatures around the throne reveal the four mighty powers on the earth: the ox, the mightiest of the four-footed domestic animals; the eagle, the king among the fowls of the air; the lion, the king of the beast; and man, who was given dominion over all creation.

Man was created on the sixth day, and the number six has always been considered in biblical numbers as the number of man or mankind. When David fought Goliath, the giant was six cubits tall (1 Sam. 17:4). The Hebrew children were commanded to bow to the image in Babylon when six different types of instruments were played in unison (Dan. 3:5, KJV). The future mark of the beast is 666 (Rev. 13:18).

The number seven is alluded to in Genesis 2. When God completed His creative work, "He rested on the seventh day" (Gen. 2:2). This imagery of the number seven alludes to a cycle of rest, completion, or perfection. The *rest* cycles are: each seventh day is a Shabbat (rest); followed by each seventh year, called a Sabbatical cycle; followed by seven years of seven sabbatical cycles (forty-nine years). In each cycle of seven days, seven years, or seven cycles of seven years, the people, animals, and the land rested (Lev. 25:1–7).

The use of seven in representing completion or perfection can be seen in the seven seals, seven trumpets, and seven vial judgments in Revelation (chapters 5, 8, 15). Jesus spoke seven sayings from the cross before completing His redemptive work. The word *seven* or *seventh* is used 583 times in Scripture and is always linked to the things of God, the kingdom of God, or the prophetic future as it relates to God.

One other number commonly found in the Bible is the number forty. This number has represented a period of testing. It is alluded to in the story of Noah's flood, where the rain fell for forty days and nights. After the rain concluded, Noah experienced a second period of testing as he waited in the ark an additional forty days before the dove returned with an olive branch. Later we read where Goliath taunted the Hebrew army for forty days before being slain by David. Christ was tempted of the devil for forty days in the desolate Judean wilderness! Clearly, the number forty is a number of testing and chastisement; Israel wandered through the wilderness for forty years—one year for every day that they doubted God!

THE MEANINGS OF COLORS

The law of first mention is also found in the presentation of colors, metals, and fabrics found in the Scriptures. When Moses was building the tabernacle in the wilderness, God instructed him to use purple, blue, red, and white dyed fabrics. Without entering into a detailed study of the fabrics of the tabernacle, blue is heavenly, purple is royalty, red is redemption, and white is righteousness. A scarlet (purple) robe was placed on Christ at His trial while the soldiers mocked Him as the king (Matt. 27:27–29). A red cord was hung in the window of the harlot Rahab's apartment, marking her house for redemption and protection from destruction (Josh. 2:17–18). In heaven, the saints will wear white robes, which represent the "righteousness of the saints."

When it comes to metals, three are mentioned frequently in the Scriptures: gold, silver, and brass. Gold is the most precious, representing deity. Gold never tarnishes, never needs cleaning, is eternal (never aging), and just as God is sinless, never needs to repent of any sin. Silver is a precious metal that represents redemption. Under the old covenant, a silver shekel was collected from all men over twenty years of age, called the *shekel of redemption*. The entire collection was placed in the temple treasury and was used for repairs of the tabernacle and, later, the temple in Jerusalem. When Jews celebrate the yearly Passover, four silver cups are used for the fruit of the vine, each cup representing an aspect of the redemption from Egypt.

BIBLICAL SYMBOLISM

Some of the most common forms of symbolism found in Scripture are animals that are used to identify nations or individuals. You may wonder why Scripture uses the animal kingdom as symbolism so frequently. I believe the simple answer is that God used what the people of ancient history were most familiar with. The same could be said of Christ's outdoor teaching ministry. When Christ spoke of a man sowing seed in a field, the wheat and tares, and the thorns, His Galilean audience was completely familiar with the objects He used in His famous illustrated messages.

The biblical symbolism of objects and animals is similar to the symbolism of numbers, metals, and colors in that the first mention of the object or thing usually sets the pattern for the cryptic, mystical, or symbolical understanding of that particular object or thing.

The first created creature that became prominent in the Bible was the serpent, which was "more cunning than any beast of the field which the LORD God had made" (Gen. 3:1). Notice that the Bible does not use a term like "reptile" or "slithering thing" but places the serpent with the "beast of the field." Today when we think of a beast in a field, we picture a large ox, a bull, a cow, or other large animal that roams in the field. However, the serpent was more than a skinny snake. He was subtle or crafty and was also able to communicate in some manner with Adam and Eve. Because a serpent initiated the first deception, the fallen angel, Lucifer, called the devil and Satan, became a picture of a deceiving serpent. In fact, he is called a serpent in Revelation 20:2.

One of the most commonly mentioned animals in Scripture is the lamb. The word *lamb* or verses using the word *lamb* first appear in Genesis 22, where Abraham predicted that God would "provide for Himself the lamb" (Gen. 22:8). However, the main story of a lamb that connects this precious creature with Christ is the Passover narrative recorded in Exodus 12. A perfect pet lamb was chosen from the flock. Its blood was sprinkled on the left, right, and top post of the outer door of each Hebrew home, forming an invisible hedge that restrained the destroying angel from taking the firstborn Hebrew. The entire lamb was then roasted, and all parts were eaten by the family prior to departing from bondage to their homeland. This was not just an exodus but also a redemption from bondage and slavery. It was a preview of coming events—when Christ would appear as the "Lamb of God" taking away the sins of the world (John 1:29). In the Book of Revelation, the word *lamb* is used twenty-seven times, and in all instances but one (Rev. 13:11), the lamb is Christ.

The Bible uses other symbolism that is often found in a spiritual dream. In the Bible we read of wheat and tares. The wheat alludes to the good seed that produces children of the kingdom, and the tares are the bad seed that produces the children of the devil (Matt. 13).

There are certain animals that I call the "odd flock." They are the sheep, goat, and pig—each representing a different type of believer. The sheep always refers to believers or individuals who faithfully follow the shepherd. Sheep are never spoken of in a negative manner in the New Testament and are to be protected, loved, and cared for by their spiritual shepherd. On the opposite end are the goats. Goats are actually a part of the flocks in the Middle East, but they are separated from the sheep, as they can become difficult to get along with at times. A goat can allude to someone in the flock who has a negative attitude or refuses to obey the instructions of a shepherd. As a youth, I knew members in churches where my father was the shepherd who were definitely *goats*. They were always causing some type of difficulty through their stubborn and stiff-necked attitude. The other creature is the pig. In Judaism, a pig is considered a very unclean animal, and religious Jews will not eat any form of pork. In 2 Peter 2:20–22, a pig is a metaphor used to describe a backslider, or someone who returns to their old filthy ways.

Most believers know that the Holy Spirit is symbolized as a dove, and for good reason, when we compare a natural dove to the characteristics of the Holy Spirit.

One form of dove is pure white in color, which represents the purity of the Holy Spirit. A dove is an affectionate bird that expresses its emotions through cooing. It is also a gentle creature, a perfect imagery of the gentleness and affection of the Holy Spirit. When a dove is attacked, it does not retaliate but simply cries in distress. Believers who are filled with the Holy Spirit are instructed never to retaliate against our enemies. The Holy Spirit makes intercession for us in prayer with "groanings" (Rom. 8:26).

The great Christian minister Vance Havner once pointed out that a dove has nine main feathers on each wing and five main feathers on its tail. It is noted in Scripture that there are nine gifts of the Holy Spirit (1 Cor. 12:7–10) and nine fruit of the Spirit listed in Galatians 5:22–23. The tail feathers are similar to the rudder of a plane and assist in guiding the dove in flight. The five feathers would well be a picture of the fivefold ministry of apostle, prophet, pastor, teacher, and evangelist—the fivefold ministry provided to the body of Christ (Eph. 4:11–12). The dove is also unique from other birds because instead of its wings pointing toward its tail, they actually point toward the head. The Holy Spirit does not speak of Himself but points believers to Christ.

In the parables, the field where the harvest grain is maturing is symbolic of the world itself. Water is symbolic of the Holy Spirit when He is manifesting within the life of a believer, as indicated when Christ compared the infilling of the Spirit to someone with living water flowing from their innermost being (John 7:38).

When a believer experiences a spiritual dream with the meaning veiled with symbolism, the meaning of the dream can be understood by using the Scriptures to interpret the symbolism. On occasions I have heard sincere individuals attempting to bring understanding to a dream that was actually nothing more than a strange dream. There was no order, no instruction, and no biblical symbolism. It reminds me of the woman in my father's church who said to him, "Pastor, I had a strange dream. I saw the congregation here at the church, and instead of having normal heads, they all had large, round cabbages sitting between their shoulders." With concern on her face, she inquired, "What do you think this means?"

Dad paused and in a serious tone replied, "Sister, I believe you had too much pizza before you went to bed."

I recall a self-acclaimed dream interpreter interpreting the dreams that people phoned in. From a purely biblical standpoint, most of the dreams made no sense. Yet the person in charge made every dream a spiritual revelation and had the most elaborate system for interpretation that I had heard. However, the colors he used were totally opposite of the biblical patterns, and at that point I realized he was stretching the meanings in order to provide some form of comment for each caller.

In a spiritual dream that is meant as a warning, it is common to see serpents, wolves, tares, dark clouds, hurricanes, fish, churches, and other symbols that are used in the Bible.

THE EFFECTS OF A SPIRITUAL DREAM

When the king of Babylon arose from his dream of the metallic image, we read:

> Now in the second year of Nebuchadnezzar's reign, Nebuchadnezzar had dreams; and his spirit was so troubled that his sleep left him.
>
> —DANIEL 2:1

During my many years of ministry, one common factor in any warning or instructional dream from the Lord was the fact that after waking up, I could not go back to sleep. The dream continually remained with me for days, weeks, and months. A warning dream remains in your mind and spirit. At times there were parts of the dream that I could not remember, but I always recalled the major details of the dream or vision. I have learned by experience that the average nightly dream will occur and often be forgotten after awaking or before the day concludes. For example, last night I dreamed, but at this moment I cannot recall any details, in part or in whole, of the dream. However, a dream from God will remain in your mind or spirit for long periods of time.

WRITING DOWN WHAT YOU SEE

King Nebuchadnezzar's prophetic dream of the metallic image was so dramatic, yet when he awoke, he could not recall what he had dreamed. When Daniel began his explanation, the king remembered all of the details and exalted Daniel in the kingdom (Dan. 2). I have discovered by experience that the moment you awake from a dream, and you believe it may have a spiritual connotation, it is important to write it down on paper. For many years I have kept either a notebook or paper and a good pen on the nightstand beside our bed near the lamp. At numerous times I would awaken after dreaming or actually hearing a word or phrase spoken in my ear, and I would turn on the lamp, grab the pen, and begin to write down the word or the events seen in the dream.

On the other hand there were a few occasions that I would awaken and think, "I will remember that in the morning," as I was too exhausted to get up and make the effort to record the dream. Sadly, there were times when I awoke and could not recall the details that may have been a significant part of the meaning of the dream. Occasionally that day I would be traveling and would see or hear something that would trigger my memory, like a small light from a flashlight suddenly appearing in a dark room. The small *memory jolt*, however, was not enough to bring any substantial light to reflect on the dream.

If you are spiritually sensitive, you should keep a notebook and pen close to you at all times, even when traveling. You may be in the presence of someone who will speak a word during a spiritual or biblical conversation that will be exactly what you need to hear. The best avenue of recall is to write the insight on paper or in a journal. I have three offices, two in ministry facilities and one at home. In each location are numerous file cabinets with drawers stacked full with notebooks and notes from thirty-four years of ministry. To this day I will occasionally pull a stack of white or yellow notepads and muse over the handwritten nuggets on the paper. At countless times I have gleaned a phrase, a title, or a series of outlines from notes that were written years earlier.

I have more than sixteen Bibles that I have used over the years when preaching in revivals and conferences. In each Bible the inside and backside pages are filled with small handwritten notes and nuggets, some of which were deep words I heard in my spirit in prayer. In 1979 I was a teenager traveling in Virginia and ministering in revivals. While I was in Richmond preaching, a youth group gathered around me and began praying for my protection and for a major spiritual breakthrough. Suddenly I grabbed a pen and wrote in the back of my Bible, "The Lord says that you will see the great breakthrough in three weeks!" The next meeting was in Pulaski, Virginia, and the revival continued for three weeks. At the conclusion it was said to be one of the greatest revivals in the church's history, and it was also the revival that opened the door of opportunity for me to minister in other states. To this day I see the small inscription in the back of my old Bible, and I can recall all of the details of that moment and weeks following—all as a result of writing it down!

At times you will personally receive a special word from the Lord, and at other times someone you have confidence in will receive a warning or an instruction for you. If you are a husband, that person is often the one person closest to you—your wife.

TELLING OTHERS YOUR DREAMS

In the event of a spiritual warning or a dream with spiritual symbolism, a person must exercise wisdom and discretion when sharing any dream with a second or third party. When Joseph related his double dream to his father, Jacob, his dad successfully interpreted the meaning, since Jacob himself had experienced spiritual dreams (Gen. 37:10). However, when the lad told his brothers, he was ridiculed and mocked, and they envied him, eventually selling him as a slave, all because of his dreams (Gen. 37:8, 11, 26–28).

Believers are at different levels of spiritual understanding and maturity, just as children are at various levels. There are some children who reach age twelve and are as mature mentally and emotionally as if they were eighteen. Others reach eighteen and are as mature as a twelve-year-old! This was true in biblical times, as we see when Christ was twelve years of age and confounded the doctors of the law at the temple (Luke 2:42–47). Believers are either *milk drinkers* or *meat eaters*. The milk drinkers are the babes in Christ who are unskilled in the Word of God and must hear the simple and basic teachings from Scripture (Heb. 5:13). The meat eaters are those who understand the deeper knowledge of the Scripture, such as the major biblical doctrines, the Hebraic roots of the faith, the prophetic teachings, and other subjects that require deep and detailed study and biblical research, which produces spiritual growth.

I suggest the one thing that a new convert or *babe in Christ* should not immediately do is begin his or her study of Scripture in the books of Daniel or Revelation! However, anyone who has been raised under strong *meat* teaching should have at least a basic understanding of the symbolism found in these apocalyptic books. New believers need to understand their relationship with God and how to pray, worship, and walk by faith before engaging in the in-depth study of things to come.

I recall years ago sharing a major spiritual dream with my son, who I thought would be interested in hearing the unusual warning I felt the Lord had given me. He became quite despondent and discouraged after I shared this warning with him. Later I realized that this type of dream was not intended to share with a young man who was attending high school and had limited understanding or, for that matter, little interest in some strange warning given to his father. As my son, he interpreted the dream as just more *negative stuff* that Dad was seeing. This was an important lesson for me. He needed to be encouraged and built up as a young person. On the other hand, I sat down with my father and shared the same word, and he interpreted the meaning and began to pray about the information the Holy Spirit had revealed through the dream. The difference between these two reactions is the spiritual and emotional maturity level of the person.

You may have a dream that something bad is going to happen to someone. The last thing to do is to worry the person by screaming over a phone demanding he heed the warning before it is too late. The first thing to do is what Daniel did when he received a troubling vision or dream: he set his heart for prayer and understanding. (See Daniel 9.) Pray first before sharing this type of dream. Now, if a person comes to you with his or her dream and asks for a possible meaning, then you have more freedom and permission to search for the understanding. When I was eighteen, I was earnestly seeking God during a fast, and the Holy Spirit revealed to me many forms of ministry I would use to reach entire nations. All of the words He gave me then have since come to pass after thirty-four years of ministry. I was so excited, and I recall that at ages eighteen and nineteen I sat with other groups of ministers and told them what I saw and felt that the Lord would accomplish through my efforts. Some read this *revelation* as some form of pride or arrogance, which was not in my heart. Their response and actual rejection of the information could have discouraged me. Wisdom later taught me that it is not wise to publicly tell all the *secret things* God reveals to you. When the angel told Mary she was pregnant, she went to the one person who would understand her strange circumstances, her cousin Elizabeth (Luke 1). After all, can you imagine Mary, an unmarried virgin, running through a Jewish community yelling, "I'm pregnant! I saw a vision of an angel, and I'm pregnant, and the Lord did it—*the Lord did it*"? First, who would believe it was the *Lord alone* who helped her conceive? Second, imagine how Joseph would have been persecuted and Mary forever rejected if the community thought she was pregnant out of wedlock! There are times to make information known and times to hide and ponder things in your heart (Luke 2:19).

If you have a believing spouse, it is always good and in order not to hide *personal secrets* from one another, but to have such a trusting relationship that you can share with each other your personal feelings, desires, dreams, and visions—both visions and dreams of your plans and destiny, and visions or dreams that are messages from heaven.

thirteen

FOUR TYPES OF SPIRITUAL VISIONS

Then the LORD answered me and said:

"Write the vision
And make it plain on tablets,
That he may run who reads it.
For the vision is yet for an appointed time;
But at the end it will speak, and it will not lie.
Though it tarries, wait for it;
Because it will surely come,
It will not tarry."

« Habakkuk 2:2–3 »

When I say the word *vision*, what comes to your mind? There are several ways in which this word is used in the English language. The common meaning is a person's eyesight, or their ability to see. The second most common usage deals with an individual or a church's plans for the future, as in: "We have a vision for the future; we are going to build a new facility." This meaning of *vision* alludes to the ability to imagine, or create a plan or idea for the future, and to make it occur. However, the spiritual meaning of the word *vision* from the prophetic and biblical stories is far deeper than the two meanings above.

There are three Old Testament prophets who mention the word *vision* more frequently than other prophetic books. They are Isaiah, Ezekiel, and Daniel. In Isaiah, the word *vision* is mentioned in seven verses. In Ezekiel, it is referred to thirteen times, and in Daniel, the word is mentioned twenty-two times—more than by any other prophet. Among the prophets, a vision was a divinely inspired visual scene that a prophet saw either during prayer, during sleep, or at times when they were wide-awake. The wide-awake vision is perhaps the most rare and unusual. We read that the prophet Balaam saw "the vision of the Almighty, falling into a trance, but having his eyes open" (Num. 24:16, KJV).

Many of these visions were so remarkable that they are difficult for the average human mind to comprehend. When King Uzziah died, Isaiah saw into the heavenly throne room where the seraphim were flying above God's throne, each with six wings: two were covering their eyes, two were covering their feet, and two they were using to fly (Isa. 6:2). On the other hand, Ezekiel saw a whirlwind coming from the north, with the appearance of a fire descending. Within it the prophet saw the throne of God being carried on the shoulders of four cherubim. On several occasions Daniel saw Gabriel and numerous other strange symbolism as he witnessed beasts rising up, representing empires.

There are four different types of words found in Daniel to describe the different methods by which a vision can be received.

1. The word chazown

This word refers to a *mental sight, dream, revelation, or oracle*. It is found in Daniel 1:17, where it states that Daniel had "understanding in all visions and dreams." It can also be found in Daniel 8:1–2, 13, 15, 26, and in other references.

2. The word chezev

This Aramaic word simply means *sight or vision*. This word is used in Daniel 2:19, when Daniel received a secret from the Lord in a night vision and was later brought before the king and interpreted the famous dream of the metallic image. This form of a vision occurs while a person is asleep.

3. The word mar'ah

This word, found in Daniel 10:7–8, is also translated as "vision," and is used to describe *seeing a reflection in a mirror*. Daniel was near the river Hiddekel in Babylon when he was suddenly overtaken with a shaking that brought him to his face. He then saw what is considered in theology as a *theophany*, the appearance of Christ in the Old Testament. The man Daniel saw in the vision was clothed in linen held by a golden belt. His eyes were like lightning, his arms and his feet like brass, and his voice like the sound of many waters. Parts of this description are parallel to John's vision of Christ in Revelation chapter 1!

4. The word mar'eh

The fourth word means *sight or appearance* and is used in Daniel 10:1 where Daniel had received a vision but did not have the understanding. He privately fasted for three complete weeks and broke through the spiritual opposition that existed in the atmosphere where a demonic prince of Persia was restraining the revelation from reaching him. (See Daniel 10:1–12.)

The various words indicate that visions occur in different ways. In the Scriptures, the prophets would be in exile near a river when suddenly the inspiration of the Spirit would overcome them, and they would be "caught up" in spiritual ecstasy. John was on the isle of Patmos surrounded by the Aegean Sea when he was "in the Spirit" on the Lord's day (Rev. 1:10). To be "in the Spirit" indicated to suddenly be into the very mind of thinking of God Himself!

Ezekiel was a political prisoner in Babylon near the river Chebar when suddenly the heavens opened, and he saw the visions of God. The prophet describes the occasion as "the hand of the LORD was upon him there" (Ezek. 1:3). The seer then describes in detail the appearance of cherubs carrying the throne of God and how they traveled, moving like a "wheel within a wheel" (vv. 1–28). These are called "open visions," since they occur when the visionary is fully alert, awake, and aware of his physical surroundings. Most scholars would agree that this is the highest form of ecstatic revelation. The prophets were living on a higher dimension of holiness and sanctity, which enabled them to move from speaking to their fellow men to immediately being carried away in the Spirit into the mystical realm of the cosmic heavens and the throne of God.

The next dimension of visions is when the prophets were asleep, and they received an open vision in the night:

> In the first year of Belshazzar king of Babylon, Daniel had a dream and visions of his head while on his bed. Then he wrote down the dream, telling the main facts. Daniel spoke, saying, "I saw in my vision by night, and behold, the four winds of heaven were stirring up the Great Sea.

And four great beasts came up from the sea, each different from the other."

—Daniel 7:1–3

At times it may be difficult to distinguish between a dream and a
vision. These revelations of the four beast empires occurred while the
prophet was asleep, in a dream stage, and yet is seen in his vision.
He is asleep and yet seems awake at the same time. These dreams/
visions occur when a person is sleeping.

The fourth type of vision is the unfolding of spiritual insight that
emerges within the mind while a person is completely awake. This is
more common, and often a person may not recognize when it occurs.
Every person, especially when young, spends time daydreaming. This
can cause disruptive behavior during school hours, as the child is
present in body but absent in mind. Children may be sitting behind
a desk, and at the same time, mentally they are back home in the
yard, perhaps splashing in their plastic swimming pool. This is not
a vision but simply the imagination at work. The human mind has
the ability to create images (the root word for imagination) and can,
with a simple change in the brain, take you to any place in the world
where you can shop at the finest boutique, dine in world-class restaurants, and rest under silk sheets—all without paying a dime!

At the same time, a Spirit-filled believer can begin to meditate
upon the Lord and pray while sitting at a desk, walking down a sidewalk, or lying in a bed. Suddenly the believer may sense a strong
feeling that something is wrong. The weight of the thought presses
into his or her spirit and creates a burden. As the person begins to
pray, he visualizes a situation about which he knows nothing. As
he further enters into deeper intercession, the believer realizes he is
praying for a particular family member or a negative situation. Later,
the situation he visualized is proven true. This is a form of a spiritual vision.

This occurred many years ago when I was visiting in Oregon at a state park with an extinct volcano that was in the middle of a large lake. That afternoon I did a foolish thing, and instead of following the established walking trail to the boat dock, I went in the opposite direction and ended up on the back side of this extinct island volcano. I came to an opening where volcanic lava once flowed into the lake. It was as slick as glass, and I began falling. Lying on my stomach, I was holding on with the fingers of my hand clawing into the hard surface. I knew I could face death and began praying.

The following week I learned that on the same day, at the same time I was in danger, my father and mother were driving through Knoxville, Tennessee. Suddenly Dad saw a sudden mental vision of me in danger, and he shouted to Mom, "We need to pray. Perry's life is in danger." Dad interceded for one hour, often crying and pleading with the Almighty that wherever I was, I would be safe. It took me one hour to get across the slick side of the island, and I knew it was prayer that sustained me.

When my wife and I were searching for property to construct a new ministry center, she and I were at our desks—I was studying, and she was engaged in bookkeeping. Without any warning I sensed that I should get out of the building and drive our van to the opposite end of town. I saw a piece of property in my spirit that I had never seen before. After convincing her that I had a word of knowledge from the Lord, we drove to a part of town we never knew existed. There we found the house we lived in for five years and the property on which we have built two major ministry centers!

THE DIFFERENCE BETWEEN DREAMS AND VISIONS

All men, women, and children are tripartite beings, consisting of a body, soul, and spirit. Dreams seem to emerge or develop more in the realm of the soul, whereas visions are deeper manifestations, which are conceived within the spirit of the person.

Whenever there is a strong outpouring of the Holy Spirit, there will always be an increase of spiritual revelation. In the last days, the Lord will pour out His Spirit upon "all flesh; your sons and your daughters..." (Joel 2:28; Acts 2:17). It is difficult to determine the actual age of a "son or daughter" from the actual Hebrew or Greek words. In most instances, a son and daughter is one who is not married and still under the influence of the parent. My son and daughter can be married and still remain my son and daughter; however, the children they have become my "children's children" or my children's "seed." Today, children who have become young adults are marrying much later than they did in my day or even my father's day.

Why would *young* men see visions and *old* men dream dreams? Why is it not reversed to read, "Young men shall dream dreams and old men shall see visions"? Does it really matter? I believe it is because the Spirit will be poured out on the youth, and this intensive movement of the Spirit always increases the intensity and the sensitivity of the human spirit to the things of God. I believe the second reason has to do with the level of spiritual maturity. Because of years of personal experiences with the Lord, the old men have their senses trained to correctly discern the spiritual from carnal, whereas a youth may not have the maturity to correctly discern or understand the deeper truth.

Young men need a vision—one so dramatic and clear that it becomes impossible for a young man to doubt it was from the Lord. An older, more experienced believer has a fine-tuned spirit and can quickly determine if the dream was from the Lord or not, and should know the symbolism in the Bible to determine the meaning of any spiritual dream.

THE IMPORTANCE OF *VISION*

In our lives a *vision* is required to bring about all possibilities and desires in our heart. To build anything, including a home, an office, a business, or a marriage, demands that the participants have some form of vision. The largest things built on Earth began with a mental image in someone's mind. The plan is transferred from the image of the mind to a blueprint on paper, followed by a team of individuals prepared to take the written design and create a visible, three-dimensional object.

▶ A visionary has the ability to see something finished before it ever begins.

▶ A visionary has the strength to call those things that are not as though they already were.

▶ A visionary continues to believe in the vision despite all opposition and hindrances.

▶ A visionary never lives in the past, but from past mistakes learns to never repeat them in the future.

There is a powerful scripture in Proverbs 29:18 that says, "Where there is no vision, the people perish" (KJV). Another translation reads, "Where there is no revelation, the people cast off restraint" (NIV). A revelation can involve insight concerning your future or your destiny as designed by God. If a doctor tells a patient that he or she has only two months to live, that patient will either resign himself or herself to face death, or the person will fight the disease to live longer. When a person feels he has nothing to live for, then a spirit of hopelessness will often grip him. Proverbs 13:12 says, "Hope deferred maketh the heart sick: but when the desire cometh, it is a tree of life" (KJV). For example, cancer patients have been known at times to extend their lives for many years beyond expectation because of *desire*—a desire to remain longer with their companions, a desire to see their grand-children grow up, and a desire to continue to enjoy life. Lack of hope can kill, but desire can become a tree of life.

A *vision* always concerns the future and seldom, if ever, the past, as God's kingdom and human life always move forward and never look backward. We cannot undo the past, but we can pursue the future. You may spend your entire spiritual walk and never experi-ence a literal night vision while in deep sleep. However, you must continually live with dreams and visions and desires to be blessed, to be a blessing to others, and to fulfill all that the Lord puts in your heart.

When Moses died, Joshua his servant filled his shoes. The Lord promised Joshua, "As I was with Moses, so I will be with you" (Josh. 1:5). About thirty years later we read these wonderful words con-cerning Joshua: "He left nothing undone of all that the Lord had commanded..." (Josh. 11:15). The purpose of a *practical* vision is to cause you to pursue your future. A spiritual vision often announces a warning to prepare you for what is coming. Always remember, a warning is never to scare you but to prepare you.

fourteen

DREAMS—AMAZING PURPOSE FOR THESE REVELATIONS

And it shall come to pass in the last days, says God, that I will pour out of My Spirit on all flesh...your young men shall see visions, your old men shall dream dreams.

« Acts 2:17 »

If you were to interview the average church attendee in North America and ask, "How does God speak to His people today?" a vast majority would reply that He no longer speaks to us except through Scripture. Of course, God's ultimate and complete revelation is revealed to mankind through the sixty-six books of the Bible. The Holy Scripture *is* God's final instruction for mankind and a revelation of His redemptive covenant through Christ. However, the reason so many Christians believe God no longer speaks to His people is because they perceive the word *speak* as being "audible words" coming from out of the atmosphere instead of God speaking to us through our own inner spirit. Since most believers have never heard an audible, deep, booming voice piercing the atmosphere, they assume God is silent—except through His written Word! Unfortunately, many Christians deny the possibility of God speaking to a person because they are continually bombarded *from the pulpit* with statements like: "God does not speak today." "God spoke only to the original apostles." Or, "We do not need God to speak since we have His Word."

A minister who denied that God speaks to anyone today was asked, "If God does not speak today, then how can any sinner be saved, since they must be convicted of their sin by the Holy Spirit?" Conviction is more than mentally agreeing with a sermon from a pulpit. It is a deep feeling of remorse that leads to repentance. Who brought that feeling? What was that still, small voice that said, "This message is for you. Believe this Word"? That was the voice of the Holy Spirit! No man can come to the Father unless he or she is drawn to Him by Christ through the Holy Spirit (John 6:65; 15:26–27).

FIVE WAYS GOD STILL SPEAKS TO HIS PEOPLE

There are five methods God uses to communicate personally to a person, if that person has the spiritual ears to hear His voice.

1. He speaks to the conscience of a person.

We are warned that in the last days there will be a release of "seducing spirits" in the earth (1 Tim. 4:1, KJV). These spirits are activated to remove men and women from the truth. As men and women are deceived and reject the truth, Paul wrote that these individuals would have their "conscience seared with a hot iron" (v. 2). This statement alludes to the effects of a hot iron upon the skin, which would cause the skin to be become rigid and hard, and the nerves damaged and dead to sensibility. The conscience is part of the human soul and reacts to a person's moral or ethical actions by judging them to be either right or wrong. A moral conscience should exist in all Christians. It also exists in many morally upright non-Christians.

Through the Holy Spirit, God often penetrates the awareness of the conscience of men and women, both converted and unconverted, and directs them in the right direction related to moral and judicial decisions. For example, when a jury of twelve sits in a box in a courtroom, listening to the testimony of a man who raped a child, even an unbeliever knows by his conscience that such an act is immoral and wrong. Something *inside him or her* tells that unbeliever that the criminal deserves a guilty decision and a penalty. Each time a sinner is converted, the Holy Spirit has pierced the mental and spiritual *veils* and spoken directly to the conscience of that individual, leading the person to Christ.

2. He speaks to the inner spirit of a person.

The Bible says, "For as many as are led by the Spirit of God, these are sons of God" (Rom. 8:14). Paul wrote about the "inward man" (Rom. 7:22; 2 Cor. 4:16), and Peter mentions the "hidden person of the heart" (1 Pet. 3:4), which alludes to the conscience and soul of each human. The human spirit is the seat of spiritual influence in the same manner that the physical heart is the center of the human body. This inward part is often identified with the phrase "the heart." This brings confusion, for the physical heart pumps blood throughout the body; thus, how can the heart discern or have thoughts?

The Hebrew Scriptures use three Hebrew words to describe the activity of the heart. The Hebrew word *chedher* is translated "reins" and refers to the deepest seat of the breast, bowels, or the deepest seat of emotions. The King James Bible uses the word *reins* (Prov. 23:16). The Hebrew words *tuchoth* and *qereba* mean the middle or the midst of the heart.[1] The ancient cultures saw the *heart* as the center of all emotions and thought. In realty, the human spirit is the seat of all emotions and a filter for all thoughts. When the Holy Spirit begins to speak to a believer within the spirit, the believer will experience strong feelings, which some call *intuition*, that bring a sense of warning, danger, or excitement concerning an individual or a situation. These feelings in the spirit can become strong burdens, which are internal weights or pressures that a person feels around the heart. A burden is often interpreted as a feeling of anxiety or stress, as it can be felt within the body.

I have learned by experience that the only way to determine if the burden or weight is a spiritual matter is by spending time in prayer and intercession. Spiritual weights can only be lifted by the hand of the Lord. After intense prayer I often sense the burden being lifted, and this becomes a signal that the Holy Spirit is moving on behalf of those things I am unaware of.

3. He speaks by using others' wise counsel.

The Bible says, "Where there is no counsel, the people fall; but in the multitude of counselors there is safety" (Prov. 11:14). A counselor is an advisor who gives advice to resolve conflicts, to instruct in business, or to warn about and weigh possible dangers. Solomon, king over Israel, understood that: "For by wise counsel you will wage your own war, and in a multitude of counselors there is safety" (Prov. 24:6). In the Old Testament, kings like King Ahab surrounded himself with *yes-men* and false prophets who were hired for pay and enjoyed dinner at the king's table. It was difficult for such men to warn the king or rebuke him when he was wrong, as negative words were not accepted and often led to a long month in chains in a dungeon under the palace. (See 2 Chronicles 18.)

Often a person on the outside of a situation can see more clearly than those within the organization or situation, because their vision is not blurred by numerous opinions. Many years ago I was engaged to be married to a talented, young woman whom I had dated steadily for about two years. For some reason, everyone who personally met her did not feel that she was the *right one* for me. If only two or three people had indicated this, I would not have thought too much about it. However, this became consistent for months. We both agreed to break off the engagement, and I later married a wonderful young woman named Pamela and have been in love for more than thirty years!

The individuals *counseling* me were on the *outside looking in,* but it did not mean they were not properly discerning my situation. When we become emotionally linked to a person or situation, our focus becomes narrowed, and we are unable to view the broader field of play. At times the Holy Spirit can and will bring a person to speak into our situation, one who is speaking not only the will of God but also giving us possible warnings to avoid a pitfall or a trap that could be set by someone close to us. If you are preparing to become engaged, I suggest some godly wisdom before making a life-changing decision! If you are beginning a business, don't jump just because it looks good. Weigh the positives and negatives, and remember that the Holy Spirit can direct someone to you with a word in season. Isaiah wrote:

> The Lord GOD has given Me
> The tongue of the learned,
> That I should know how to speak
> A word in season to him who is weary.
> He awakens Me morning by morning,
> He awakens My ear
> To hear as the learned.
>
> —ISAIAH 50:4

4. God speaks today using the vocal gifts of the Spirit.

I realize that there will be some reading this section who will disagree with my comments, based upon your church tradition, denominational persuasion, and personal experiences. However, when the Holy Spirit was given as a gift to the body of Christ (Acts 2:38–39), He brought with Him nine fruit of the Spirit (Gal. 5:22–23) and nine gifts of the Spirit (1 Cor. 12:7–10). I find it interesting that ministers believe in the Holy Spirit as a person but teach that the miraculous gifts listed in 1 Corinthians 12 have somehow ceased in our time. Yet they still believe and teach that all nine fruit of the Spirit are for our time!

Paul wrote that the "gifts and the calling of God are irrevocable" (Rom. 11:29). Once God has issued a gift for the body of Christ, He will not withdraw that gift. We are also informed that we should "come short in no gift, eagerly waiting for the revelation of our Lord Jesus Christ" (1 Cor. 1:7). These verses indicate that the gifts (Greek, *charisma/charismata*) are given and will continue until the return of Christ—despite what is being taught in some circles of unbelief.

The three main vocal gifts mentioned in 1 Corinthians 12 are *different kinds of tongues, interpretation of tongues,* and *prophecy.* I have personally witnessed my precious father, Fred Stone, on numerous occasions as he began praying the prayer language of the Spirit and was understood by a person from another nation who spoke the same tongue my father was praying in! In the early 1970s, Dad pastored in Arlington, Virginia. One particular Sunday, a medical doctor, Dr. Spence, and his wife, Mary Ann, were visiting our little church on Fillmore Avenue. That morning Mary Ann came forward for prayer for a special need. As Dad prayed for her, he began praying in the prayer language of the Holy Spirit. After prayer, Mrs. Spence looked at him and asked, "Where did you learn to speak such fluent German?" Dad replied that he had never studied German, but this was the prayer language from the Holy Spirit. She and her husband were amazed. Dad had spoken in perfect German, praying for her and even giving details about her family that only she knew! This incident so impressed this couple that they began attending Dad's church and became wonderful members!

I cannot recall the number of occasions when an operation of one of the vocal gifts—either through a direct word to a foreigner (1 Cor. 12:10), an interpretation of a tongue (1 Cor. 14:1–5), or a prophetic word of encouragement and edification (v. 3)—were manifested in the church and brought spiritual warning, insight, and comfort to the church, as well as a "sign...to unbelievers" (v. 22). Because these gifts operate through human vessels, the words given must be judged by others in the church who have experience and wisdom in spiritual matters and are grounded in the Word of God (v. 29). No word that is truly from the Holy Spirit will ever contradict the sound teaching from the Bible! However, God can and will use humble and godly vessels through which to let His gifts flow.

5. God speaks through dreams and visions.

I was amused recently when a near relative was witnessing to another individual about the deeper things of the Holy Spirit. My relative was informing this particular *spiritual unbeliever* of how the

Lord had warned me on several occasions about events that would come to pass in the nation, including my 9/11 vision of the twin towers and the dream-vision of the oil crisis in the Gulf of Mexico off the coast of Louisiana. This skeptic said he did not believe that God spoke to anyone in our day in any fashion except through the Bible. The relative then asked, "How do you explain Perry's receiving these warnings, which were so direct and clear that it could not be denied that they were 100 percent accurate?"

The answer was, "He has some type of psychic powers!" I was amazed that according to this man, a person could have some type of counterfeit power, but God was helpless to use His own power to reveal the future!

These same accusations were thrown at Christ when He performed miracles. The religious Pharisees accused Him of being possessed with a demon and of performing His miracles by the power of Beelzebub (Matt. 12:24). This lie was intended to frighten the multitudes from following Christ, as no one wants to be associated with anyone operating through a demonic influence.

The Bible teaches that in the last days God will pour out His Spirit upon all flesh, and this deluge of God's presence will be accompanied by "your young men shall see visions, your old men shall dream dreams" (Acts 2:17). Today's prophetic ministers continually remind people that we are in the *last days*, pointing out numerous prophecies related to the "last days" to undergird their statement. However, these same men cannot avoid this *Acts 2* promise from the Lord. To indicate that a particular verse is a "last days prophecy prediction for our time" and then turn around and say, "But this verse in Acts is not for today," is not only spiritually dishonest, but it also hinders people from believing God will reveal warnings and personal instructions in visions and dreams!

GOD COMMUNICATES WITH US
THROUGH DREAMS AND VISIONS

For four thousand years of biblical history, from Adam to the Christ, God revealed insights and revelations to holy men through visions, dreams, and mental inspiration. The agent of these revelations was the Holy Spirit. That same Spirit is covering the earth today as nations of hungry individuals study the Word of God and see events that will come to pass through the means of visions and dreams. God still speaks today!

The Book of Job introduces Job as the "greatest of all the people of the East" (Job 1:3). His wealth portfolio included houses, land, seven thousand sheep, three thousand camels, five hundred female donkeys, and five hundred yoke of oxen. He was blessed with ten children and servants (Job 1–2). Satan planned a strategy against Job with the intention of destroying his integrity and causing him to profane and curse God (Job 1:10–11). During the attack Job lost all his children, their homes, and all of his material wealth. In a second wave of assault from the adversary, Job was stricken with boils and endured severe physical trauma (Job 2:7).

From the moment of his attack, Job sought for answers to the enigma of why the righteous suffer. Three friends visited Job during his loss and engaged in a long discussion about life, faith, and suffering. It is evident that Job was seeking God for a divine revelation to his dilemma. As we read the narrative, there are some eye-opening passages that reveal how God speaks to men.

> Now a word was secretly brought to me,
> And my ear received a whisper of it.
> In disquieting thoughts from the visions of the night,
> When deep sleep falls on men,
> Fear came upon me, and trembling,
> Which made all my bones shake.

Then a spirit passed before my face;
The hair on my body stood up.
It stood still,
But I could not discern its appearance.
A form was before my eyes;
There was silence.

—Job 4:12–16

The first point is the use of the phrase "deep sleep." There are many passages in Scripture about a prophet who was being given a divine revelation from a visit of the Lord that indicate the prophet entered a "deep sleep." In Genesis 15:12, a deep sleep came over Abraham as the sun was going down, and the Lord spoke to him. In Daniel 8:18, Daniel remarks that he was in a "deep sleep with my face to the ground" when the angel of God touched him. He repeats the same concept about deep sleep in Daniel 10:9. After he entered this deep sleep stage, he heard the words of a messenger of the Lord.

Just what is a "deep sleep"? The Hebrew phrase can allude to being "sluggish" or entering some form of a "spiritual trance." In my own life, there have been several times when I experienced a true spiritual vision. Usually I was extremely exhausted when this occurred. I believe that this tiredness sometimes causes the fleshly or carnal man—who is always busy and going nonstop—to be more suppressed, thereby enabling the inner spirit of a person to become more alert or aware.

NOW I LAY ME DOWN TO SLEEP

Sleep is a very important part of living a long life. When a person is under stress or mental anguish, it is difficult to rest. A continual lack of sleep is called *insomnia*. A person who sleeps but continually tosses and has difficulty breathing may have *sleep apnea*. Excessive sleep, to the point that a person wants to sleep and not get up, can be symptomatic of *narcolepsy*. All three of these forms of sleep disorders are very unhealthy and should be treated. These disorders not only interrupt normal sleep patterns but can also cause irregular and bizarre dreaming patterns to occur.

During normal sleep, there are five stages of sleep that a person will enter. The first is the drowsy stage, which, with most people, will last a period of about ten minutes. This is followed by a second stage of light sleep, where the heart rate decreases along with a decrease in the body temperature. This state is followed by the third and fourth stages, called "deep sleep," in which the body enters a deep sleeping state and the brain waves begin to slow down. The fifth stage is called *REM* (rapid eye movement) sleep, characterized by eye movement, increased respiration rate, and increased brain activity.[2] This last stage is considered the dream level, when most people dream.

I have discovered that visions can occur at any given time, but dreams usually occur during the time of deep sleep, usually between two to five in the morning. Dreams always transpire when sleeping, whereas a vision can occur with a person's eyes opened. (For more information on visions, see chapter 13.)

THE EAR IS OPENED

The inspired writer of Job speaks of the "ear" being opened to receive a secret word in Job 4. If a person has normal hearing, he will receive all information through the avenue of hearing. We all have physical ears; however, there are also *spiritual ears*. Your physical man has the capability to hear and dissect information, but we must have a spiritual *inner ear* to correctly hear the revelation of the Word of God and the voice of the Holy Spirit! This fact is clear when reading about the seven churches in Revelation. Repeatedly the writer says, "He who has an ear, let him hear what the Spirit says to the churches"

(Rev. 2–3). The fact that Christ had to repeatedly instruct His own followers (church members) to pay attention and hear indicates that there can be hearing problems that arise with your spiritual ear—or spiritual discernment. Our natural ears are always *turned on*, but our spiritual ears also need to be continually open.

When we are physically asleep, an amazing thing occurs. The human ear is able to close out any small noises and allow the mind to enter into rest. Of course, any sudden or loud noises can immediately shock a person out of a deep sleep! I have been with a group of people driving in a vehicle when one of the passengers fell asleep. Others would carry on the conversation, but the sleeping passenger heard nothing that was said. This idea of hearing and dreaming is unique, especially as it relates to someone with a physical disability.

WHAT ABOUT A COMA VICTIM?

For many years the medical community has been curious as to the neurological activity occurring in a person who is comatose, or in a coma. A coma is usually caused by a traumatic head injury, often through a fall or an accident. The person appears to be inactive, like they are sleeping. It is noted that at times a comatose individual will have a muscle reaction, such as twitching or squeezing a person's hand. Doctors often inform hopeful family members that this is simply a muscle reaction and not an indicator of the person's response.

One of the interesting aspects of a person in a coma is that if the auditory nerve that runs from the brain to the ear is still intact, it is quite possible for the injured person to actually hear the conversations that are occurring around them. In 1998, my beloved grandfather John Bava was taken to surgery in Elkins, West Virginia. He experienced three strokes, which affected his brain, and he was never able to move, open his eyes, or communicate again. However, his doctor told us to speak directly in his ear, because hearing was the last thing to go when a person was dying! The family placed a cassette player near his bed and began playing his favorite gospel songs. The heart monitor showed his heart beat going from a low 60 beats a minute to as high as 120 beats a minute when the music was playing. When the room was quiet, the heart rate slowed dramatically. When he heard our voice, our singing, or the music, his heart rate immediately increased. I knew he was unable to move, but I also knew he could hear us speaking. His brain may have been impacted by three strokes, but his inner spirit was alive, and he heard—not just with his natural ears but also with his spiritual ears!

I found it interesting that when a person is about to depart this life, under normal circumstances their hearing is the last physical responder to cease. This is important information for any family member standing near the deathbed of a dying loved one. If that individual never made a public profession of faith, then the believer should speak into his or her ear and instruct the dying loved one to pray a prayer in his or her mind. As long as the spirit has not departed from the physical shell (see 1 Corinthians 5:3; 2 Corinthians 5:6), God knows the "thoughts and intents of the heart" (Heb. 4:12) and can hear a prayer of repentance prayed from a person's mind. In the Bible we read where it says, "Jesus, knowing their thoughts..." (Matt. 9:4).

Richard Madison, a minister friend of mine, was in a terrible head-on collision on April 13, 1986. He was rushed to the hospital and was pronounced brain dead upon arrival. Due to numerous serious injuries and broken bones, he remained in a brain-dead coma for twenty-seven days. His Christian mother would come into his room every four hours and anoint him, believing God to raise him up—which God did! Richard describes how on one occasion his soul came out of his body and walked down the hall of the hospital, going to the hospital chapel where his mother and others were praying. He could hear his mother praying, and he actually stood beside her, watching her pray as she asked the Lord to "save Richard and bring him out of the coma." It was at that moment—while he was out of his body—that Richard prayed and asked Christ for help! On another occasion he actually heard a nurse use profanity and rebuke him for being in the coma. She was upset because it was New Year's Eve, and she had to work that night and was going to miss a party! Imagine her shock when Richard woke up out of the coma and walked out of his wheelchair ten weeks later. When he recovered, he told the nurse her entire conversation in his room that New Year's Eve! Despite the coma, Richard's soul and spirit could still hear the words and voices in the room from time to time.

The writer in Job said that when a person went into deep sleep, his "ear received a whisper of it" (Job 4:12). Even in sleep there is an *inner ear* linked with the spirit of an individual, which continues to hear. This is the *ear* that the Lord uses to give His instructions. This is the reason Christ addressed the seven churches in Revelation by saying: "He who has an ear, let him hear what the Spirit says to the churches" (Rev. 2:7).

A second passage in Job reveals several unique reasons, seldom discussed, why God gives His followers a dream:

> For God may speak in one way, or in another,
> Yet man does not perceive it.
> In a dream, in a vision of the night,
> When deep sleep falls upon men,
> While slumbering on their beds,
> Then He opens the ears of men,
> And seals their instruction.
> In order to turn man from his deed,
> And conceal pride from man,

He keeps back his soul from the Pit,
And his life from perishing by the sword.

—Job 33:14–18

The first reason given is that God "seals their [man's] instructions." The Hebrew word here for *instructions* means an *admonition* or some form of *direction*. This passage was written about the time of Moses, before the entire Bible was ever compiled and the written Word of God placed in the hands of common men. Some ministers who refuse to believe that God can still speak today to and though His people would suggest that God no longer uses visions and dreams, since we have the Bible and these visionary methods were ancient, *pre–New Testament methods*. These ministers should consider the following:

- ▶ Does the Bible specifically tell you the woman that you should marry—other than a believer?

- ▶ Does the Bible reveal which life occupation you should pursue—other than to be a witness to others?

- ▶ Does the Bible reveal the place you should live—other than living by faith?

- ▶ Does the Bible reveal where you should serve Him— other than to always be a giver to the kingdom?

- ▶ Does the Bible tell you if you should drive, fly, or avoid that trip you are planning?

The Bible is God's inspired Word, and it gives us promises, prophecies, and practical teaching for living on Earth while walking with God. However, there are many practical aspects in life that must be discovered through prayer and intercession or through a word of wisdom or knowledge (1 Cor. 12:7–10), including a word of instruction given in a dream or vision. It was a dream that opened the door for Joseph to initiate a plan of provision in the time of famine!

The second purpose of a dream or vision is to turn us from our own direction ["deed"] to the direction of God. A dream or vision can reveal God's will or plan for your life. When the wise men came to Jerusalem, inquiring of Herod as to where the Hebrew prophets said the Messiah would be born, Herod consulted the religious Pharisees, who in turn reported back that Bethlehem was the anticipated town. Herod instructed these Persian Magi to return to him once they knew of the whereabouts of the infant child (Matt. 2:8).

After a visitation with the holy family, the wise men were returning to Jerusalem when an angel of the Lord warned them in a dream not to return but to depart another way (v. 12). In this instance the Lord was interrupting their prearranged plans and providing protection for them through an alternative route. The same angel would later warn Joseph to get out town with the infant Christ and His mother, because Herod was sending soldiers to slay all children under two years of age (v. 13).

Another reason for visions and dreams is to keep our soul from the "Pit" and the "sword." The pit can be the literal pit of an eternal hell, but it could also allude to a snare that is set by the enemy. The sword is a metaphor for war, fighting, and violent destruction. In Ecclesiastes 7:17 we are asked, "Why should you die before your time?" I believe it is possible to depart this life prematurely. It can occur through illegal drug addiction, alcoholism, gang-related violence, and accidents. It is possible to be at the *right place at the right time* and *the wrong place at the wrong time*. When my father was traveling to Ohio to visit his parents late at night, he stopped at a rest stop. There was one van in the parking area with tinted windows. As

Dad stepped out of his car, he had a sudden flash (mental vision) that informed him that four long-haired men were watching him from the van, and if he entered the men's room, he would be robbed and wounded. Dad immediately snapped his fingers as if he forgot something, unlocked and opened his car door, cranked up the engine, and pulled out. As he did, the van door swung open, and four long-haired men jumped out and attempted to catch up with his car but failed! Obedience to the sudden mental vision saved his life. Paul said, "I was not disobedient to the heavenly vision" (Acts 26:19). Obedience brings a positive outcome in all instances. The writer of Job taught that visions and dreams are heavenly visitations to give instructions, warnings, and directions.

Conclusion

DREAMS AND VISIONS— GOD'S VOICE OF INTIMACY

In summing up the reasons for dreams and visions, I believe that understanding the true purpose of God in revealing the future and giving instruction in dreams and visions involves four aspects of our walk with God. These four aspects are found in Genesis 22, where Abraham offered Isaac to God on Mount Moriah.

1. There is the plan of God.

2. There is the place of God.

3. There is the provision of God.

4. There is the purpose of God.

THE PLAN OF GOD

The Bible says, "For I know the thoughts that I think toward you, says the LORD, thoughts of peace and not of evil, to give you a future and a hope" (Jer. 29:11). We are also told that our thoughts are not God's thoughts and our ways are not His ways (Isa. 55:8). God desires to make His thoughts toward you known, and He does this primarily through His Word (v. 11). However, there are practical plans for us that must be known to us.

In Genesis 22:1 the Lord initiated a plan that would test Abraham's faith and obedience. God instructed, "Take now your son, your only son Isaac, whom you love…and offer him there as a burnt offering" (v. 2). This was the plan—to offer Isaac. When the Lord brings a spiritual revelation to you, it is for the purpose of a plan. He may not always give you the reason why He is asking you to attend a certain church, take a missions trip, work with children, give a special offering, and so forth, but obedience always involves His plan.

When Abraham led Isaac three days away from home to the land of Moriah (v. 4), notice who was missing from the story—Sarah was not present. The reason is obvious. Isaac was actually in his thirties at the time and was so attached to his mother that he had not met his future wife or gone on his first date! If Abraham would have informed Sarah, saying, "The Lord spoke to me to take Isaac and offer him up as a sacrifice," a war would have broken out, and Sarah, no doubt, would have prevented Abraham from following through with the act. This is why you don't always tell everyone your vision until the right time. God's plan always comes in vision form, whether it is a literal vision, a mental vision, or a dream vision that you see in your spirit.

THE PLACE OF GOD

God had a plan, but He also had the place. Abraham was to go to the land of Moriah and offer Isaac on one of the mountains that the Lord would show him (Gen. 22:2). The land of central Israel in and around Jerusalem is surrounded by mountains—but God chose a specific mountain! Years before Isaac's birth Abraham had offered tithe to the first king and priest of the Most High in Jerusalem—Melchizedek (Gen. 14:20; Heb. 7:9). Thus, the areas of Moriah and

Jerusalem were set apart as holy to the Lord and to Abraham. It was a special place, a place marked by God. The phrase "the place" is found in Genesis 22:3–4, and 9.

As a believer, you can be at the right place at the right time, the right place at the wrong time, and the wrong place all of the time, unless you know God's will for your life! When Moses was discouraged with Israel's sins in the wilderness, he desired to see the glory of the Lord, and the Lord said, "Here is a place by Me" (Exod. 33:21). Moses entered a cleft of the rock and experienced the glory of the Lord when he entered the "place" God had marked (vv. 22–23). Hundreds of years later, a depressed prophet, Elijah, ran to the same mountain (Mount Horeb) and entered a cave, where he experienced the still, small voice of the Lord instructing him (1 Kings 19:8–12). I personally believe that Elijah found the same cave—that "place"— where Moses had met with God hundreds of years before.

God's blessing for you will be discovered when you find your *place* in His purpose. God spoke in dreams and visions to the early patriarchs, directing them from one place to a different place. As they sought out that special place, they found themselves in the center of the will of God.

GOD HAS THE PROVISION

Our generation is very *provision* oriented. Often believers will accept any type of promise or blessing, try any type of prosperity package, and seek out someone who has an alleged anointing to pray finances into their lives. A need being met is for the present, but the meaning of provision is to provide, prepare, or supply something for future needs. Men and women express their concerns about having the proper provisions for the future.

When God tested Abraham on Mount Moriah, the loving father carried the knife for the sacrifice and the fire for the altar, and Isaac carried the wood to the top of the mountain (Gen. 22:5–6). Once they reached the top of the mountain, Abraham built the altar. Just before Abraham pierced his son with a dagger, the angel of the Lord stopped the process and pointed to a ram that was caught in a thicket by its horns (vv. 9–13). This ram would become the provision for Abraham and would become a picture of the future sacrifice of a lamb that would one day become the final offering for all mankind upon that same mountain (vv. 7–8).

Notice in the narrative that this ram was caught in a thicket by the horns. This is interesting, as at this time Abraham was more than 135 years of age, based upon the age of Sarah at her death in Genesis 23:1–2. It would be difficult for such an old man to wrestle with a ram if that ram was free and not caught in the thicket. In fact, any ram could have outrun Abraham, had he attempted to chase it down. By catching this large animal in the thicket, God took the *fight* out of the blessing!

When you have discovered the plan and found the place, there will always be provision at that place, and God will take the battle out of the blessing. The provision is at the place, and the place where you should be is revealed from the Scriptures and through the inward leading of the Holy Spirit and at times through visions and dreams.

GOD HAS A PURPOSE

This is the divine order: the plan, the place, the provision, and the purpose. Abraham was unaware of the ultimate purpose of this test at the time. However, because God's covenant man, Abraham, was willing to give up his only son to God on the altar (Gen. 22:12), God Himself would one day give up His Son as a sacrifice on the cross for man's redemption (John 3:16). In this narrative Abraham somehow received either a vision of God's plan and purpose, or it was revealed to him as the Bible records: "And Abraham called the name of the place, The-LORD-Will-Provide; as it is said to this day, 'In the Mount of The LORD it shall be provided'" (Gen. 22:14). I am uncertain what Abraham saw or experienced that day. However, he did predict that "God will provide for Himself the lamb" (v. 8).

In the New Testament, Christ was referring to this incident when He said, "Your father Abraham rejoiced to see My day, and he saw it and was glad" (John 8:56). The purpose of this test concerned the future. The entire scene on Mount Moriah in Genesis 22 is a picture of what was to come with the crucifixion of Jesus Christ!

We all have a tendency to want to know the purpose or the reason *first*. We ask: "Why must I do this, Lord?" "Why are You leading me to this, Lord?" "Why help this person?" On and on the questions of *why* continue. We are motivated to obey if we know the purpose. However, if we knew why, we would not be walking by faith—we would be walking by sight (2 Cor. 5:7). If the Holy Spirit revealed the details of what was coming to you, both the good and the bad, you would try to speed up the good and would intervene to prevent the bad. When God brought Israel out of Egypt, He never told them about the walled cities, the giants in the land, and the seven Canaanite tribes they would need to conquer until they went in to spy out the land. God knew that if the people were aware of the coming battles, they would resign themselves to remain in Egypt and destroy the destiny of the children and their nation! Thus God only reveals the future in bits and pieces, or, as Paul said, "We see in a mirror, dimly" (1 Cor. 13:12). The purpose can only be revealed after we have followed the process!

Our personal lives must be rooted and grounded in the Word of God. Dreams or visions or even prophetic words and spiritual gifts are not intended to replace the inspired Word of God. They serve as complements to the teaching and preaching of the Scriptures and act as tools for the Holy Spirit to assist in directing us during special seasons of our lives. However, a person should never despise these spiritual visitations and must learn to properly discern them. I hope this book has helped you in this matter. God bless you.

Appendix

DETAILED BIBLICAL SYMBOLISM IN DREAMS

This section will present numerous objects and symbols found in the Scriptures that are also part of a spiritual dream. I will give the first place in Scripture where the word is found and give a generally possible meaning of each word. Please understand that the general *meaning* may not be the only meaning but is the most common possible meaning.

OBJECT: ARROWS

First Reference: Numbers 24:8—Moses wrote that God defeated His enemies by using arrows.

Possible Meaning: We no longer use a bow and arrows, but arrows were used in battle to defeat the enemy.

Just as a sword can represent the Word, the individual arrows being shot can be a cryptic reference to individual scriptures that are quoted and *shot* toward the enemy. They become the *arrows of God* in the hands of a mighty man. If someone is shooting an arrow at you to harm you, it may be destructive words that are being said (Ps. 64:3–4; Jer. 9:8). If the arrow pierces your body, especially in your heart, it can represent words that are spoken to bring pain to your heart and spirit.

OBJECT: BIRD(S)

First Reference: Genesis 15:10—Abraham sacrifices birds without dividing them on the altar.

Possible Meanings: In the Bible, birds are not always viewed positively. When the birds ate the food from the basket on the head of the baker, Joseph said the head of the man would be removed by Pharaoh and the birds would eat his flesh (Gen. 40:17–22). In the New Testament parable of the sower and the seed, the birds come to eat the seed as soon as it is planted in the heart of a person. Christ said these "fowls" (birds) were evil spirits (Mark 4:1–20). Birds eating seed can represent something that is attempting to steal the Word from your heart. Birds are also used as a metaphor for evil spirits (Rev. 18:2).

In a dream, if a bird is picking at your flesh, it can mean that you will encounter difficulty with your flesh, either through temptation or through a physical ailment. If the bird is pecking your home, it can refer to something or someone working their way into your home that will become a problem for you later.

OBJECT: BOATS/SHIPS

First Reference: Genesis 49:13—Jacob predicted Zebulun would be a haven for ships.

Possible Meaning: We think of traveling when we think of a ship or a boat. In the New Testament, many of the disciples were fishermen who owned their own boats (Matt. 4:21–22; Luke 5:3–7). Because fish were caught in nets and boats transported the catch, boats can allude to the ministry vessel used to bring in the souls. The boat is the vehicle used to minister.

OBJECT: BREAD

First Reference: Genesis 3:19—God said man would eat his bread by the sweat of his face.

Possible Meaning: Bread is a basic staple that sustains life, especially among empires of antiquity. In the New Testament, Christ taught that we should pray for our "daily bread" (Matt. 6:11). Bread can allude to the Word of God (Matt. 4:4). Christ is called the "bread of life" (John 6:35). While bread can be literal food or refer to the food supply, in a spiritual dream, bread is the gospel that feeds the multitudes and satisfies the soul of a person.

OBJECT: BULL

First Reference: Genesis 32:15—Jacob's list of animals consisted of ten bulls.

Possible Meanings: A bull can be an aggressive beast. In Psalm 22:12, the writer said the "strong bulls of Bashan have encircled me." A bull can be a type of an aggressive spirit or a situation that will cause you agitation. I once dreamed of many bulls running during a crisis, and it alluded to the stock market whose emblem outside of Wall Street is a brass bull.

OBJECT: CATTLE

First Reference: Genesis 1:24—Cattle are listed by name on the fifth day of Creation.

Possible Meanings: In the Bible, cattle were significant with personal prosperity, as they were the chief desired beast of the field. They are mentioned 151 times in the King James Version of the Old Testament. They were used for milk and meat. Joseph saw seven strong, then seven weak cattle, indicating a coming famine. Cattle can allude to your personal or business prosperity.

OBJECT: CHAINS

First Reference: Genesis 41:42—Pharaoh put a gold chain around Joseph's neck.

Possible Meanings: In the Old Testament, a chain has two meanings: the first is where a gold chain is placed around the neck of a leader (Dan. 5:7); the second is where chains are placed upon someone to bind him (Lam. 3:7; Ezek. 16:11). The man of Gadara was bound with chains (Mark 5:3). Peter was bound in prison in chains (Acts 12:6–7), and fallen angels are bound in chains (2 Pet. 2:4).

In a dream, someone in chains can refer to a bondage of some sort that is binding the individual. If you are in chains, it can illustrate an attempt of the adversary or individuals to place you in some type of spiritual bondage, captivating or binding you. If the chains are on your feet, they mean a hindrance in carrying the gospel. On your hands, they are stopping the work you are doing. If they are over your mouth, they are attempting to silence you.

OBJECT: CORN

First Reference: Genesis 27:28 (KJV)—Isaac blesses Jacob, telling him he will have plenty of corn and wine.

Possible Meanings: The King James translation of the Bible (1611) uses the word "corn," and in the West we think of tall stalks of corn in a cornfield. The Hebrew word is *dagan*, and refers to grain. In the West, however, corn is a main grain that is grown nationally for food, fuel, and other purposes.

In the 9/11 vision in 1996, the five grayish tornadoes took out five rows of corn. In this instance, it was a prediction that the economy would be impacted by these storms, as corn being grown, sold, and eaten is a part of our national and global economy. Thus, a field of corn is still a harvest, but it can allude to the economic impact of a certain event upon the area seen in the dream or vision.

OBJECT: DESERT

First Reference: Exodus 3:1 (KJV)—Moses is on "the backside of the desert" watching sheep.

Possible Meaning: Israel wandered through the wilderness/desert for forty years because of unbelief (Deut. 2:7), and Christ was tempted of the devil in the wilderness for forty days (Matt. 4:1–2). Evil spirits are said to walk "through dry places" (Luke 11:24). A dry desert can refer to a time of trial or temptation that will be encountered. It can also mean isolation and a period of loneliness and standing alone in your faith.

OBJECT: DOG

First Reference: Exodus 11:7—God said not even a dog would move against the children of Israel.

Possible Meanings: In America, dogs are pets. David rebuked Goliath for considering David a "dog" (1 Sam. 17:43). Among Jews in Christ's day, Gentiles were considered "dogs" (Matt. 15:26). Paul wrote, "Beware of dogs" (Phil. 3:2), which were evil-minded people. In ancient times, dogs were mostly without masters, wandered around, and were considered unclean. In a dream, a filthy dog is an unclean person, and a vicious dog is a violent person.

OBJECT: DOOR

First Reference: Genesis 4:7—God told Cain that "sin lies at the door."

Possible Meanings: If the door is locked, it indicates a closed opportunity or a hindrance to your progress. An opened door is an open opportunity or the opening you should travel (Rev. 3:8; 4:1). In my dreams of churches, sometimes there are no doors but only openings like a doorway. This indicates that Christ Himself is the door to the church (John 10:9).

OBJECT: EARTHQUAKE

First Reference: 1 Kings 19:11—Elijah experienced an earthquake that shook the mountain.

Possible Meaning: A dream of an earthquake can be very literal, as the first simple interpretation. An earthquake is a shaking that causes disruption and damage, depending upon the magnitude of the quake. In a spiritual dream, an earthquake can refer to a sudden and unexpected shaking that will occur. If you are in a church, it may not be the physical building but the body of believers who will experience a shaking. Earthquakes divide land, and a severe spiritual quake could mean a division of some sort is in the future.

OBJECT: A FIELD

First Reference: Genesis 2:5—God speaks of the herbs and plants in the field.

Possible Meanings: Ancient Israel was built upon agriculture and planting cycles. The fields were used for barley and wheat (Deut 8:7–10). In the New Testament parables, the field is the world and the harvest is the souls of men who are represented by the wheat and the tares (Matt. 13:38). In several dreams and visions in the past, I have seen large fields, some with grain and some without. In these cases, it represented the entire United States as a whole. In one instance there were piles of grain stacked in the field with a Bible on top. However, grain was still standing in the corners. This, of course, was the gleaning of the fields, which occurs at the very end of the harvest cycle (Lev. 23:22).

OBJECT: FIRE

First Reference: Genesis 19:24—God rained down fire on Sodom and Gomorrah.

Possible Meaning: Fire is referred to 549 times in the KJV translation of the Bible. In many instances it is used to describe a judgment (Gen. 19:24), fire for a sacrifice (Gen. 22:6), or refers to God as when He manifested in the form of fire (Exod. 13:21–22). Isaiah's lips were cleaned by coals of fire from the altar (Isa. 6:5–7). Uncontrolled conversation (the tongue) is compared to a fire (James 3:5–6). Certain types of trials and temptations are called "fiery trials" (1 Pet. 4:12).

A fire can refer to a trial, negative words being spoken, a purging of someone, or some situation that is going to occur.

OBJECT: FISHING

First Reference: John 21:3—The disciples were fishing after the resurrection of Jesus.

Possible Meanings: Fish are mentioned in both Testaments. Ezekiel speaks of spreading nets to catch many fish (Ezek. 47:10). Several of Christ's disciples were fishermen and lived in fishing communities (Luke 5:1–7). Christ said He would make them "fishers of men" (Mark 1:17). In a dream, fishing is usually an indication of ministry and reaching souls. If the lake is small, it is a smaller ministry; if large, a large church or ministry is indicated. A fishing pole symbolizes a local church ministry, but a net indicates a global impact.

OBJECT: FLOWERS

First Reference: Exodus 25:31—Flowers are mentioned when describing the gold menorah and the beaten gold flower design on top.

Possible Meanings: Flowers appear once the winter is past and the spring arrives (Song of Sol. 2:11–12). Flowers indicate a fresh beginning, a passing of the old, and initiation of the new with a season of refreshing and rest. Flowers that have not bloomed indicate the early or infant stages of the new beginning.

OBJECT: FOXES

First References: Judges 15:4—Samson caught three hundred foxes, using them to set the Philistines' fields on fire.

Possible Meaning: Foxes are small animals known to be crafty and subtle. They sneak in, do their damage, and then get out before being detected. Song of Solomon speaks of the "little foxes that spoil the vines" (Song of Sol. 2:15). A fox can represent a person who is working behind your back, unnoticed by you, but slowly hindering what you are doing by what they are doing. By "spoiling the vines," the spiritual growth or flow of the Holy Spirit is being disrupted and the fruit that should come forth will not manifest.

OBJECT: GOAT

First Reference: Genesis 15:9—God required Abraham to offer a she goat as an offering.

Possible Meanings: Goats were used twice to deceive. First, when Jacob placed goat's hair on his arms, posing as Esau to deceive his father (Gen. 27:16), and second, when Joseph's coat was dipped in goat's blood and presented as a sign that he was slain by an animal (Gen. 37:31). A goat is a negative image in the New Testament and can represent someone who is in the flock of sheep but is not real and can be deceptive by nature. The sheep and goats will be separated at the judgment (Matt. 25:33).

OBJECT: JEWELRY OR GEMSTONES

First Reference: Genesis 24:53—Rebekah was given jewelry of silver and gold from Abraham's servant.

Possible Meanings: Jewelry or gemstones were handed over from the Egyptians to the departing Hebrews, who used the gold, silver, and jewelry for the building of the tabernacle in the wilderness (Exod. 11:2; 12:35; 35:22).

At the believer's judgment, good works will be rewarded with "gold, silver, and precious stones" (1 Cor. 3:12).

To dream or see precious stones or precious metals is a good sign that there is coming a great blessing in some form, including but not limited to financial blessing or rewards for your faithfulness. This is what most believe will be a part of the reward.

OBJECT: LAMB

First Reference: Genesis 22:7–8—Abraham predicted God would provide a lamb for the offering.

Possible Meanings: Throughout the Bible, a lamb symbolizes the ultimate sacrifice, Jesus Christ (John 1:29). Jesus, the Great Shepherd, told Peter to "feed My lambs" (John 21:15). Thus, lambs in a spiritual dream indicate a flock of believers or the church.

OBJECT: LAMP

First Reference: Genesis 15:17—God passed between Abraham's sacrifice with a burning lamp.

Possible Meaning: A lamp provides light in darkness. The commandments and the Word of God are compared to a lamp (Ps. 119:105; Prov. 6:23). In the parable of the ten virgins, all had lamps, but five virgins lacked the additional oil and had no light when the call came (Matt. 25:1–8).

A lamp burning is a sign that the light of the Word is present. A lamp gone out can allude to the light or truth not being presented or received.

OBJECT: LEFT HAND

First Reference: Genesis 13:9—Abraham tells Lot to chose between the left and right side of the land before them.

Possible Meaning: In Job 23:9, Job recalls God's blessing and his present trials and implies that although he cannot see God, when he is on God's left, God is at work with His left hand. Some rabbis teach that God created light with His left hand and darkness with His right. The left hand refers to a time of trial or seasons where it may appear that God is not working for us.

OBJECT: LIGHTNING

First Reference: 2 Samuel 22:15—Speaks of God's power, which includes sending lightning to discomfort His enemies.

Possible Meaning: The meaning of lightning depends on the setting and circumstances in a dream. When lightning strikes in the natural, it can cause fires and destruction, can shut down power, and so forth. In a spiritual dream, if lightning is striking on a clear day, it can indicate a coming storm that you do not see at the time. If striking during a storm, it indicates the violent or very troubling events that will unfold during the time of the spiritual storm.

OBJECT: LIMPING/INJURY

First Reference: Genesis 32:25—The angel touched Jacob and his hip socket was out of joint permanently.

Possible Meaning: In his earlier days, Jacob was on the run, but with a limp he was slowed down, and it caused him to depend more upon God than upon himself. When experiencing a limp, it means something that will affect your spiritual walk.

The people of Israel were warned that if they followed the Canaanite idols, these false gods would become "scourges on your sides and thorns in your eyes" (Josh. 23:13). If a person has a moral failure, that person receives a form of a limp.

OBJECT: LOCUSTS

First Reference: Exodus 10:14—God sent a plague of locusts to the Egyptians.

Possible Meanings: Locusts devour anything that is green and growing. A swarm can wipe out plants and the leaves of trees (Exod. 10). A locust is an insect that if not destroyed can slowly destroy entire crops (Joel 1:4). Locusts are small, but when joined as a swarm, they are a great agitation.

In a spiritual dream, a locust is a small creature and can be the imagery of small things combining together to agitate and create many hindrances that you need to battle. You need to protect the spiritual growth in your life and guard against letting little things agitate and become big destroyers.

OBJECT: MEAT

First Reference: Genesis 27:4—Isaac asked Esau to prepare his favorite "meat" (KJV).

Possible Meanings: In the KJV, meat is first used in Genesis 1:29: "Every tree...shall be for meat." This word in Hebrew is *oklah* and means food. The word *meat* in Genesis 27:4 refers to actual animal meat, which is the main meaning throughout much of the Bible. In the New Testament, the two levels of understanding and receiving the Word of God are "milk and meat" (Heb. 5:12–13, KJV). Milk is the simplicity of the Word received by immature or young believers, whereas meat is the stronger doctrine of the Scriptures.

Dreaming of meat in a spiritual dream can allude to the deeper teaching or instruction from the Word of God or to more mature believers.

OBJECT: MOUNTAIN(S)

First Reference: Genesis 7:20—The flood waters prevailed above the mountains during Noah's flood.

Possible Meanings: Mountains have numerous applications. Sitting or living on a mountain can allude to a great victory or accomplishment, as the ark "rested" on the mountains of Ararat (Gen. 8:4). Being at the bottom of a mountain and attempting to climb can allude to a situation that will take time and effort to deal with. Mountains can be difficulties that need to be removed by faith (Matt. 17:20). The seven mountains in prophecy are seven major kingdoms of prophecy (Rev. 17).

OBJECT: OIL

First Reference: Genesis 28:18—Jacob poured oil on top of a rock to mark the spot of visitation by the angel of the Lord.

Possible Meanings: Throughout the Bible, oil became the substance used to mark a sacred spot or to anoint sacred objects, including kings, prophets, and priests (Exod. 28:41; 1 Sam. 16:12; Zech. 4:14). James instructed the elders to pray over the sick, "anointing him with oil in the name of the Lord" for their healing (James 5:14). Oil is a very positive symbol in a spiritual dream and is linked to ministry, the anointing of the Spirit, or the calling of God for His work and service.

OBJECT: PROSTITUTE

First Reference: Genesis 34:31—Simeon and Levi are angry that their sister was treated like a harlot.

Possible Meaning: In the Old Testament, a harlot is a symbol of religious unfaithfulness and spiritual adultery. In Revelation 17, a harlot is riding on the beast representing the final kingdom. To dream of a harlot indicates seduction from the truth or turning from righteousness. The seduction can come through a person or through a spirit that will rise and work against your mind and your beliefs.

OBJECT: RAIN

First Reference: Genesis 2:5—In the Garden of Eden, the Lord had not yet caused it to rain on the earth.

Possible Meaning: With the exception of the flood of Noah (Gen. 7–8), rain by itself (without flooding or lightning) is a good indication of the blessing of the Lord in your life, ministry, or church. The terms "early and latter rain" refer to the outpouring of the Holy Spirit (Joel 2:23; James 5:7). A businessman once dreamed of supporting our ministry and of gold raindrops falling upon him. As he did begin to support our ministry, his business began to flourish and prosper. Rain also brings growth and fruit to plants and trees.

OBJECT: RIGHT HAND

First Reference: Genesis 13:9—Abraham told Lot to choose the land between the right and left hand.

Possible Meaning: The Genesis 13 reference deals with deciding between two choices. Later in the ancient culture, the right hand represented authority or power. The mother of James and John wanted Christ to seat her sons on His right hand (Matt. 20:21). Christ is in heaven seated at the "right hand of God" (Acts 7:55–56). Christ has seven stars in his right hand (Rev. 1:20), and the seven-sealed book is in the right hand of God (Rev. 5:1, 7).

The name *Benjamin* means "son of my right hand," as the right hand is symbolic of having favor, receiving authority, and position.

OBJECT: RIVER

First Reference: Genesis 2:10—In the Garden of Eden, four rivers flowed from one source to water the garden.

Possible Meanings: One of the famous biblical rivers is the Jordan in Israel, mentioned 182 times in the Old Testament in the King James Version. It serves as a border between two nations: Israel on the west and Jordan on the east. When the Jordan was crossed, it represented a new beginning, as Joshua crossed with Israel (Josh. 3–5). Elijah crossed the Jordan and was translated (2 Kings 2:6–13), and Christ was baptized in the Jordan (Matt. 3:13). Crossing the Jordan also alluded to a picture of death and resurrection.

If a river is flooding in a destructive manner, it can indicate a literal flood or a flood of difficulties. If it is dark water, it is a trial, but clear flowing water in a river can indicate a coming transition that will be smooth.

OBJECT: ROCK(S)

First Reference: Exodus 17:6—Moses stood upon the rock in Horeb to bring forth water from the rock.

Possible Meanings: Scripture teaches that God is our rock (Deut. 32:4) and that the rock that brought forth water in the wilderness was Christ (1 Cor. 10:4). Stumbling on a large rock can represent a spiritual offense either in the Word or an offense caused by believing in Christ (1 Pet. 2:8). A rock foundation means a strong spiritual foundation in the Word of God.

OBJECT: SAND

First Reference: Genesis 22:17—God promised Abraham that his seed would be as the sand upon the seashore.

Possible Meaning: The stars are heavenly, but sand is earthly. The "spiritual seed" of Abraham is the church, whose promises are heavenly. The earthly seed are the natural Hebrew people, as their promises from God are earthly (the land of Israel, Jerusalem, and so forth). Stars can *fall from heaven* (which is what occurred with Lucifer, Isaiah 14:12–15). Sand can also be shaken by wind and moved by water. Christ taught that any foundation built upon the sand will eventually collapse (Matt. 7:26–27).

To dream of sand presents several possible meanings. Walking in sand is to walk into, or through, a possible unstable situation. To be buried in sand is earthly, indicating carnal surroundings that are attempting to choke you spiritually. To build on sand indicates one who "hears these sayings of Mine [Jesus], and does not do them" (Matt. 7:26).

OBJECT: THE SEA

First Reference: Genesis 1:26—Man was given dominion over the fish of the sea.

Possible Meanings: In prophetic application, the sea can allude to nations of the earth (Isa. 17:12). The beast of Revelation 13:1 rises up from the sea, or from the nations around the Mediterranean, called the Great Sea in Daniel (Dan. 7:1–4). When Daniel saw the winds "stirring up the Great Sea," it was indicating conflict among the nations (v. 2).

OBJECT: SERPENT

First Reference: Genesis 3:1—The serpent in the garden tempts Eve to eat from the forbidden fruit.

Possible Meanings: Satan used the serpent in the garden, and thus throughout the Scripture a serpent is the imagery of Satan or the powers of darkness. In Revelation, Satan is called "that serpent of old, called the Devil" (Rev. 12:9; 20:2). A spiritual dream involving serpents is never a good omen and alludes to an attack or a very difficult time. If the serpent bites you, it means the problem will have an effect upon you emotionally, physically, or spiritually.

OBJECT: SMOKE

First Reference: Genesis 19:28—Smoke "like the smoke of a furnace" want up when the cities of Sodom and Gomorrah were burning.

Possible Meanings: Smoke is the result of a fire. Smoke is never a positive imagery because it represents the remains of something that has burned. David spoke of being "like a wineskin in smoke" (Ps. 119:83), referring to a wineskin hanging in a tent near a fire that the smoke dries out.

Smoke can create discomfort and block what you are attempting to see. Where there is *smoke there is a fire*, and this can refer to a situation that creates stress and confusion.

OBJECT: STARS

First Reference: Genesis 1:16—God made the lesser light such as the moon and stars.

Possible Meanings: Stars are imagery of lights that shine in darkness. They also symbolize eternal promises such as when God said that Abraham's seed would be as the stars of heaven (which cannot be numbered, Gen. 15:5). Seeing stars often represents the promises of God, especially provision during dark or difficult times.

OBJECT: STORMS

First Reference: Job 21:18—The writer of Job speaks of how a storm carries away the chaff with the wind.

Possible Meaning: Scripture speaks of escaping the storm (Ps. 55:8), of God being a covering, or shelter, in the storm (Isa. 4:6), and of God performing His will through a storm (Nahum 1:3). In the Gospels, storms would arise on Galilee; one nearly capsized the boat of the disciples (Mark 4:37; Luke 8:23).

A spiritual storm that God allows can help a person search his or her life and remove the excessive chaff from the life of a believer. A storm created by your circumstances will cause you to search your life to determine your spiritual level of faith. A storm created by demonic powers is intended to capsize your faith, as when Satan desired to sift Peter as wheat to destroy his faith (Luke 22:31–32). A storm in a dream indicates conflict, a time of difficulty, or a challenge that is come into your life, family, or church. If it damages trees, it can allude to individuals getting hurt because of the situation.

OBJECT: SWINE

First Reference: Leviticus 11:7—God classifies the swine as an unclean animal.

Possible Meaning: In the New Testament, the evil spirits in the man of Gadara went into the swine (Matt. 8:32). Christ instructed His followers not to "cast your pearls before swine" (Matt. 7:6). In 2 Peter 2:22, a backslider is like a dog returning to its vomit and a swine that is washed returning to the mud. In a dream, a swine is a very unclean person or situation and can allude to a backslider who once knew Christ but has returned to his or her life of sin.

OBJECT: SWORD

First Reference: Genesis 3:24—The cherubim with flaming swords were guarding the tree of life in Eden.

Possible Meaning: This flaming sword was a picture of the future power of the Word of God. Ephesians 6:17 teaches that the "sword of the Spirit" is the Word of God. Hebrews 4:12 says the: "word of God is quick, and powerful, and sharper than any twoedged sword" (KJV).

I've had numerous dreams of using a double-edged sword, and in every instance I was using it to fight a spiritual adversary—meaning I would defeat the adversity by reading, quoting, and believing the Word of God.

OBJECT: TORNADOES

First Reference: 2 Kings 2:1—Called a "whirlwind" in the Bible, tornadoes are mentioned twenty-seven times in the Old Testament.

Possible Meanings: A whirlwind is very sudden and very destructive, and it always represents either a literal storm of sudden disaster that is coming or a spiritual storm. Each time I have dreamed of a tornado it was a sudden disaster, often on a national level. I saw the five tornadoes in the 9/11 vision in 1996 and the oil tornado in the Gulf of Mexico in July of 2007.

Jeremiah 23:1–20 mentions the destruction caused by whirlwinds, which would also cause many deaths. Jeremiah was possibly alluding to the swiftness of the Babylonians who entered Israel and wreaked havoc on the temple and the city of Jerusalem. I once saw a leader over the U.S. State Department who was being followed by three huge tornadoes; I knew it represented three major nations or national problems she would deal with in her administrative position.

OBJECT: TREE(S)

First Reference: Genesis 3:2—Eve spoke to the serpent concerning the trees in the garden.

Possible Meanings: Trees actually have several meanings. Literal fruit-bearing trees can allude to success (if they have fruit, Ps. 1:3) or to economic and business difficulties (if they are withered, Joel 1:12). An individual tree could also allude to a person, as when King Nebuchadnezzar saw a large fruit tree cut down to the ground and Daniel interpreted the dream to mean that the tree was the king, and he would be cut down for seven years (Dan. 4).

The type of tree is significant also. A palm tree represents the righteous (Ps. 92:12), and a cedar can allude to the righteous in ministry, as cedars were used in the temple (2 Chron. 1–6). A weeping willow can represent a time of sorrow (Ps. 137:1–4). A mustard tree can allude to faith (Luke 17:6), and a fig tree has prophetically alluded to Israel as a nation (Hosea 9:10). A barren, dead tree can allude to total death in the home, job, a person, or a situation.

OBJECT: VALLEY(S)

First Reference: Genesis 14:17–18—Abraham met the king-priest Melchizedek in the Valley of Shaveh.

Possible Meaning: Most Old Testament battles were fought in the valleys, including the battle of the five kings (Gen. 14:1–3), Joshua's fight in the Valley of Aijalon (Josh. 10:12), and David slaying Goliath in the Valley of Elah (1 Sam. 17:2). Thus, valleys can indicate a time of conflict, struggle, and some form of clash. In Psalm 84:6 we read of godly men who "as they pass through the Valley of Baca, they make it a spring." A valley is something to pass through in order to get to the next destination.

OBJECT: VESSELS

First Reference: Genesis 43:11—Jacob told his sons to take fruit, spices, and nuts to Egypt in vessels.

Possible Meaning: There are numerous references to vessels throughout the Bible. In the New Testament, Paul wrote that the spiritual character of individuals is compared to vessels of gold, silver, wood, and earth (2 Tim. 2:20). There are "vessels of mercy" (Rom. 9:23) and even vessels of wrath (v. 22). Humans are compared to vessels, as we are containers that can hold righteousness, peace, joy, and the presence of God within our spirits (Rom. 14:17). When a person dreams of a shattered vessel, it can indicate a trial that will cause great brokenness. Picking up pieces can indicate you will assist in helping heal a bad situation. A full vessel can be a full blessing. The metal gold is associated with the priesthood or ministry (Ezra 1:1–11).

OBJECT: WALKING BAREFOOT

First Reference: 2 Samuel 15:30—David left Jerusalem barefooted, running from a conspiracy to overthrow him.

Possible Meaning: Dreaming of being barefooted can represent not being prepared for a situation. David had to leave the city quickly to prevent a possible assassination (vv. 30–32). I have dreamed of being barefooted, and in each case something happened very swiftly and unexpectedly. When you wear your "gospel shoes," your feet are "shod with the preparation of the gospel" (Eph. 6:15).

OBJECT: WATER

First Reference: Genesis 2:10—Four rivers went out to water the Garden of Eden.

Possible Meanings: Throughout Scripture, water was needed for survival among the ancient tribal families. A lack of water created famines. Water usually alludes to the Holy Spirit, as when Jesus spoke of the Holy Spirit, He said, "He that believeth on me...out of his belly shall flow rivers of living water" (John 7:38–39, KJV). Water purifies, quenches thirst, and causes life to flourish—all three examples of the work of the Holy Spirit. A well of water is your inward source of blessing from the Spirit. A full well is fullness of the Spirit, and a dry well is a dry, empty spirit.

OBJECT: WEIGHT SCALES

First Reference: Job 31:6—Job spoke of being evenly weighed in God's balance.

Possible Meaning: The Old Testament uses the word "balance" when referring to scales. The Scriptures speak of a false balance (Prov. 11:1, KJV) and a just weight (Prov. 16:11, KJV). Daniel interpreted the handwriting on the wall, which said, "You have been weighed in the balances, and found wanting" (Dan. 5:27).

A dream or vision of a balance identifies God's plan to weigh something or someone to see if it is just or unjust and if the blessing or disfavor of God will rest upon it.

OBJECT: WHEAT

First Reference: Genesis 30:14—Reuben brought mandrakes from the field during the wheat harvest.

Possible Meanings: Many of the local wars that Israel fought with the Philistines and other tribes occurred at harvest time. The enemies desired the grain that had been collected. This is why Boaz was sleeping at his grain pile to prevent thieves from stealing the work of an entire month (Ruth 3:7). The wheat was very precious and valuable and sustained life for the people throughout the long winters.

In the New Testament, the wheat represents the children of God in the kingdom (Matt. 13:38). Wheat also represents the local, national, and worldwide harvest of souls who need to be reached with the gospel. In nearly every example, a full wheat field is a full harvest, a dead wheat field is an area that has been spiritually destroyed by events that have hindered the effectiveness of the gospel, and a diseased wheat field can mean that the message preached in an area has been corrupted or perverted. Gathering in grain indicates you will have an ingathering of souls. Losing grain indicates people will depart from you, your church, or ministry.

OBJECT: WIND

First Reference: Genesis 8:1—When the wind sent from God blew over the earth, it dried up the floodwaters in Noah's day.

Possible Meanings: There are two types of wind: wind that comes from heaven as a manifestation of the Holy Spirit, such as the "mighty rushing wind" on the Day of Pentecost (Acts 2:1–4), and wind that brings destruction and death, as when Satan produced the wind storms that destroyed the house of Job's family, bringing death to ten children (Job 1). In a dream, if a wind is tearing up the surrounding area, it indicates a time of severe trouble is coming. If the wind is gentle and brings a positive feeling, it can allude to a move of the Holy Spirit upon a situation.

NOTES

CHAPTER 1
THE LAST DAYS—TIME TO PIERCE THE VEIL

1. Elizabeth Dias, "In the Crystal Ball: More Regulation for Psychics," September 2, 2010, TIME.com, http://www.time.com/time/nation/article/0,8599,2015676,00.html (accessed September 14, 2010).

CHAPTER 2
THE DREAM FACTOR

1. Flavius Josephus, *Antiquities of the Jews*, book 10, chapter 7, Christian Classics Ethereal Library, http://www.ccel.org/j/josephus/works/ant-10.htm (accessed December 13, 2010).

CHAPTER 3
WHY ARE SOME DREAMS DELAYED IN COMING TO PASS?

1. Jaquetta White, "BP Oil Spill May Cost Louisiana Fishing Industry $172 million," *New Orleans Times-Picayune*, October 15, 2010, http://www.nola.com/business/index.ssf/2010/10/bp_oil_spill_may_cost_louisian.html (accessed October 18, 2010).

2. Stephen C. Fehr, "Gulf States Fear Long-Term Fiscal Effects of Oil Disaster," Stateline.org, June 24, 2010, http://www.stateline.org/live/details/story?contentId=493859 (accessed October 18, 2010).

CHAPTER 4
NIGHTMARES AND DIRTY DREAMING

1. Answers.com, "What Is the Origin of the Word *Nightmare*?" http://wiki.answers.com/Q/What_is_the_origin_of_the_word_nightmare (accessed December 13, 2010).

2. Emil G. Hirsch, "Lilith," JewishEncyclopedia.com, http://www .jewishencyclopedia.com/view.jsp?artid=421&letter=L (accessed September 15, 2010).

3. W. E. Vine, *Vine's Complete Expository Dictionary of Old and New Testament Words* (Nashville, TN: Thomas Nelson, 1984), s.v. "demon, demoniac," 158.

4. Ibid., s.v. "renewed," 960.

5. Perry Stone, *Breaking the Jewish Code* (Lake Mary, FL: Charisma House, 2009), 94–95.

6. *Israel Today* magazine, no. 75, April 2005, 12.

7. *Israel Today* magazine, no. 49, February 2003, 12.

8. Stone, *Breaking the Jewish Code*, 103–104.

CHAPTER 6
THE PSYCHIC VOICES VERSUS THE PROPHETIC VISIONS

1. William Patalon III, "Psychic Friends Network Firm Goes Bankrupt," *The Baltimore Sun*, February 5, 1998, http://articles .baltimoresun.com/1998-02-05/business/1998036093_1_psychic-friends -infomercial-bankruptcy (accessed October 7, 2010).

2. No current source information available.

3. James Henry Breasted, *Development of Religion and Thought in Ancient Egypt* (Philadelphia: University of Pennsylvania Press, 1972), 211. Viewed at www.books.google.com on October 7, 2010.

4. Adam Clarke, *Adam Clarke's Commentary*, electronic database (n.p.: Biblesoft, 1996), s.v. "Exodus 1:16."

5. Josephus, *Antiquities of the Jews*, book 2, chapter 9, http://www .ccel.org/ccel/josephus/works/files/ant-2.htm (accessed December 14, 2010).

6. Ibid.

7. Gaius Suetonius Tranquillis, *The Lives of the Twelve Caesars*, trans. by Alexander Thomson, rev. and corrected by T. Forester (n.p.: BiblioBazaar, 2008), 57.

8. Plutarch, *Plutarch's Lives of the Noble Grecians and Romans*, vol. 2, trans. by John Dryden (New York: Random House, 1992), 240.

CHAPTER 8
LEARNING TO LISTEN TO YOUR
WIFE'S WARNING DREAMS

1. *TIME*, "Worship: Gospel According to Claudia," April 12, 1963, http://www.time.com/time/magazine/article/0,9171,828101,00.html (accessed December 14, 2010).

2. Henry Forman, *The Story of Prophecy* (New York: Tudor Publishing Co., 1940), 97–98, referenced in Perry Stone, *Unusual Prophecies Being Fulfilled*, no. 7 (Cleveland, TN: Voice of Evangelism, n.d.).

CHAPTER 9
WHAT IT MEANS WHEN DREAMING
OF A DEPARTED LOVED ONE

1. Ward Hill Lamon, *Recollections of Abraham Lincoln, 1847–1865* (Chicago: A. C. McClurg and Company, 1895), 113–114. Viewed at www.books.google.com on December 15, 2010.

2. Ibid., 117–118.

3. Jill Stefko, "Abraham Lincoln and the Paranormal," April 19, 2007, Suite101.com, http://www.suite101.com/content/abraham-lincoln-and-the-paranormal-a19245 (accessed October 8, 2010).

4. Perry Stone, *Angels on Assignment* (Lake Mary, FL: Charisma House, 2009), 61–62.

CHAPTER 14
DREAMS—AMAZING PURPOSE FOR THESE REVELATIONS

1. Dwight Mallory Pratt, *International Standard Bible Encyclopedia*, electronic database (n.p.: Biblesoft, 1996), s.v. "inward part."

2. Kendra Cherry, "Stages of Sleep," About.com.Psychology, http://psychology.about.com/od/statesofconsciousness/a/SleepStages.htm (accessed October 12, 2010).